BOBBY The BABE and Me
Earl C. Fabritz
1994 Witness Productions

Published by: Witness Productions
Box 34, Church Street
Marshall, IN 47859
317-597-2487

ISBN 0-9627653-3-3

Dust cover design by: Ed Watson.

Cover Photos; (Top) Charlie Bobby in his Bobby Special in 1927. (Wilson Photo)
(Center) Babe Stapp standing along side the Duesenberg
he drove in the 1930 Indianapolis 500.
(Lower left) Herk Edwards in Gordon Webster's SR Fronty
at San Jose in 1930.
(Lower Right) Herk Edwards in 1937.
Back Cover & inside flap: The board track at Fresno, California.

Type by: The Cromer Group.

Printed in the USA.

The BOL
The BAL
and
Me

The Herk Edwards St
as told to
Earl C. Fabritz

Witness Productions
Box 34, Marshall IN 47859

Dedicated To

Charlotte

who shared in the work

and

Tom Saal

who shared the vision

Publishers Foreword

The Wisconsin State Fairgrounds presented automobile racing for the first time on September 11, 1903. Ninety years later, living in the shadows of the famous one-mile oval, Earl Fabritz works to preserve the history of the sport of auto racing.

In a few short years the last of those men who participated in the earliest days of our sport will be gone. No longer will we be able to hear first hand their gripping tales of the "Good Old Days" and get answers to the many questions we might have.

When I first read Earl Fabritz's manuscript and the words of Herk Edwards I knew that I held a precious piece of work in my hands. His stories reminded me of my great grandmother telling me about seeing the first automobile to drive through Greenfield, Indiana on the National Road and the many times I'd spent listening to my grandad tell of his days as a mechanic.

A few days ago I had the pleasure of talking to Herk Edwards on the phone. Like many of our dusty heros, who still gather in little coffee houses and restaurants throughout the country, reliving the past with old friends, the eighty-seven year old storyteller has not lost his touch. And while you may never have the pleasure of such a "bull session," perhaps this book will fill that void in your life.

It is my hope that you too will enjoy this precious little nugget of auto racing history as much as I did.

Ed Watson
Publisher

The BOBBY
The BABE
and
Me

Getting Started

When their first child was born to Walter and Mabel Edwards on June 7, 1906, in Selma, California, it turned out to be me. I was followed by my brother, Wesley and sisters, Hazel and Ethel.

My parents named me Hershel Winfred Edwards, which was quite a load for a young fellow to be carrying around. Hershel got shortened to "Herk" while I was going to grammar school. It's been "Herk" ever since and I liked it that way. When I came along, my dad was running a bicycle shop in the little town of Dinuba. We later moved to another small town west of Fresno, called Kerman, and there, my father operated a general store.

One of my earliest recollections is of my father working on his used 1908 Auburn automobile and hearing some of the choice words he used when things weren't going very well. My father got the car from a Norman DeVaux, who lived in the San Francisco Bay area and brought the car down to dad from there. I remember DeVaux and my dad engaged in a lengthy conversation concerning helicopters which had to be a visionary topic for way back then. I believe Norman DeVaux was the same man who was later involved with the DeVaux automobile.

One time we took the Auburn out to a place called Skagg's Bridge for a family picnic, and dad forgot the crank for the car. He had to borrow a fellow's saddle horse and ride back to our house to get it. Another time, the old Auburn broke down, and he had to get the loan of a team of horses and pull it the ten miles back to town. He took it to a machine shop where the engine was torn down and found to have a bad piston. They cut the old piston in half to use as a pattern, then cast and machined a new one, and had the Auburn back on the road in about a month. During that time, we went back to using a horse and buggy. Our "horse power" was a mare called Babe. She was a gentle, obedient animal and a favorite of my mother, who had a fondness for Babe that I still remember warmly.

My earliest memory of being at an auto race, was when my father took me along to see a road race that was held on the western edge of Fresno, utilizing Kearny Boulevard and Whitesbridge Road. The year was 1912, and the names Eddie Waterman, Tom McKelvey and Denta Sulprizio are still with me; either from being at the race or from hearing later discussions of it. These men were all local drivers. Sulprizio became the owner of the United Piston Company—the makers of the "Silver Lite" brand of aluminum pistons.

Our next family move involved the trade of the general store in Kerman for a ranch about half-way between Kerman and Fresno. We were there for a short while and then moved into Fresno.

In 1913 my dad became involved in the real estate business. He really needed a better way of getting around, and one afternoon, he came home in a brand new 1913 Model "T" Ford. It had a shiny brass radiator and was a joy to behold. It may have cost him the enormous sum of $350.00 or something in that range. The neighbors all gathered around to admire it and of course, dad had to give each of them a ride around the block so all could experience this marvelous machine. Dad, being the fellow he was, became a good customer of the Western Auto Store and put just about every accessory that became available on that Ford. He bought a cable type starter that was operated from the driver's seat. Sometimes you could get it started with that outfit and then again you couldn't. In any case, you always had to be careful with it so you wouldn't throw your back out of joint. This was our first experience with a new automobile, and maybe my dad overdid it, just a little.

Dad had worked up a Sunday morning ritual that didn't include going to church with my mother. He would take an oil can and a bucket of grease and proceed to give the Ford a thorough going-over. I got to watch. He'd squirt all the fittings full of grease, top up the oil cups and then do his weekly tune-up. That consisted of adjusting the vibrators on the coils and listening to them buzz. He would cock his head one way and then the other, thoroughly impressing me with the highly technical nature of that operation.

Our next family move was a mile and a half out of town on Cherry Avenue. My dad was still in the real estate business, and the miles were piling up on the Ford. One day he'd gone up into the foothills to show some property to a prospective buyer, and he was overdue getting home. When he did get home, the Ford was on the end of a rope behind another car. There was some-thing seriously wrong with the car, and it was thought to be a broken crankshaft. Dad was a mechanic of modest talents and had a few tools, but better yet, he had friends. One of them was Bill Holden, an electrician and engineer for the city of Fresno. Bill came out to talk to dad about the car. He said that if dad would tear the engine down, he would help him get it back together. Bill could only work on it in his spare time, but that was certainly agreeable with dad. So dad and I rolled the Ford under a big husky limb of our mulberry tree and went to work. We took the engine out with a block and tackle. I say "we" because I was handing him tools and trying to keep out from under his feet while listening to him expound about my lack of knowledge.

Dad took the engine apart and sure enough, it had a broken crankshaft. So he and I walked into town and went to the Ford garage to buy a new one. The fellow at the garage, who sold him the new crankshaft for $7.50, wanted to know how my dad was going to go about installing it. Dad told him he had a friend who was going to be the expert. The garage man told him it was really a job for a mechanic. "If you get the bearings too tight, they'll burn out. If you get them too loose, they'll pound out." Dad told the fellow that he and his friend could handle it. So, with the garage man's advice still ringing in his ears, dad threw the new crankshaft over his shoulder and we headed for home. On the way back, dad told me that I should watch every move that Bill Holden made and begin to learn to be a mechanic. He said the days of the blacksmith were about over, and if I became a mechanic, I'd really have a good trade. His advice that day turned out to be prophetic.

Bill Holden came out in his own car to help put the engine together. He brought his bearing scrapers and bearing blue, sat himself down and went to work. If the fire whistle from town went off, he'd have to jump in his car and hurry back to be there to cut off electrical power if that was needed. That whistle blew several times while he was there working on the motor. One time, he let me ride in with him to one of the fires which was an impressive experience for me.

When the engine was put back together and back in the car, the next thing to do was to get it started and broken in. Once it was running, they stationed me at the radiator with a can of water and instructions to keep it full. They opened a petcock on the bottom of the cooling system and sat down, carrying on a lengthy conversation. After awhile, Bill said to my dad, "Walt, I think the motor is going to be OK." They shut the motor off, waited awhile, checked the oil and then started it up again. The three of us went for a ride and my dad told his friend, Bill, that it ran better than it ever had!

A major family event in the Ford was to be a trip to the coast to get my mother away from the central valley's summer heat. In planning for the trip, a need arose for a small cargo trailer. Dad and a blacksmith friend worked out a suitable design and built the trailer. It had rubber tires and a pin-type hitch for connecting to the back of the Model "T." It took all of dad's spare time gathering the bits and pieces and helping to put it together. All of the individual parts had to be bolted or riveted together, as no welding equipment existed at that time. Once it was completed, we were on our way out of Fresno with a great feeling of escape and adventure. The first day we made it to Lemoore and stayed overnight with my grandfather at his ranch. The second day was a short one and we managed to get to Cottonwood Springs, a distance of about thirty miles. The next leg was over the "Hump" to Paso Robles. We eventually got to our final destination, Pismo Beach, after nearly a week on the road. We were happy to get there.

Along the way, we had to stop about three times for dad to reline the bands in the transmission. He got quite good at doing that. This was before what they called "quick change" bands became available. Dad left us in Pismo Beach and returned to Fresno. When the hottest days of summer were past, he returned for us. I remember that on our return trip, we carried a harvest of Pismo Clams in a tub of salt water and sand.

As time went by, there got to be more and more automobiles, and they were no longer such a novelty. My brother and I would hear them coming on the road in front of our place and we would look to see if we could identify them—sort of a little game we played. We might see a Case or a Chalmers, or an Elmore or a Hudson or a Stutz. We got so we could tell one from another at quite a distance. Of course, cars were more distinctive then, one from another, than they seem to be now, and that made it easier. On a typical Sunday, we played another little game of keeping count of the horse drawn vehicles and automobiles as they went by. The cars were gaining on the horse and buggies. The Sunday that we counted more automobiles than horses was a big one for us. We were pulling for the cars.

There was a cross road about a quarter of a mile from our place with a little country store on the corner. They had a bright red gas pump out in front where you'd pump the gas into a big bowl, up on top and then let it drain down into your tank. It seemed that every Sunday there'd be an accident there. Each driver must have thought he was the only one on the road or had the right of way. I remember one time when two cars had got into it on that corner. One of the drivers, decked out in a duster and goggles, his car crumpled up in the ditch, was pacing back and forth, fist clenched and arm raised, shouting for all the world to hear, "I had the right of way! I had the right of way!" They'd go like the wind, and since none of the cars had brakes worth mentioning, there were a lot of crashes at that corner. Many of the drivers were still on the learning curve as far as safety was concerned, and some of them were learning their lessons the hard way. We'd hear a crash and then see the neighbors heading over that way. We knew there'd been another wreck at North and Elm. Naturally, we'd have to go over too and take it all in. If it was a Cadillac and a Ford, it seemed like the Ford would make out better. It might get bent up pretty bad, but it could usually take off under its own power. The bigger cars didn't seem to survive as well.

When I was still getting around on a bicycle, I would go to the auto races and get into the infield where I could get as close as possible to the pits. I remember being there one time when Earl Cooper was running a Stutz, Art Patterson a Hudson and Ira Vail in something or other. There was a little Chevy there that day too, and he just went out there and ran away from those guys. He was flitting around there like a little mosquito and by golly he won the race! Everybody was very much impressed by that, and we were talking about it during and after the race. I heard them say it was "Dutch" Drake in the car and he was running his own cylinder head on it. Dutch's dad was John Drake, an old German blacksmith, who had a shop in Reedley. The Drake family started up the Jadson (J.A. Drake & Sons) valve manufacturing company at a time when original equipment valves left a lot to be desired. Their valves were forged from a single piece of steel and the heads didn't fall off. Later on, they made valve seats too. They later moved their business to Southern California to be closer to their market and source of supply.

Getting Started

A younger brother, Dale, was the one who got together with Louis Meyer to form Meyer-Drake and take over from Fred Offenhauser when he retired from the race engine business. Lem, another of the Drake boys, got hold of a surplus airplane after World War II in partnership with George Demron. It was in a crate, disassembled, so it needed to be put together. Neither of them were pilots or had any experience in assembling an airplane. This was to be a "learn by doing" from the ground up venture. It seems that some control wires were installed in a non-conventional manner and when Lem got the plane in the air and tried to do a certain thing, it did the exact opposite. The plane crashed in a vineyard and was a total loss. Other than bruised pride, Lem was no worse for the wear and tear, but his interest in flying made a sudden shift in other directions.

Years later, I got together with Lem and tried to find the patterns for the Chevy cylinder head that "Dutch" had made in school as a shop project. The castings had been poured in a Fresno foundry. We did find some pieces of the old patterns, but there wasn't enough there, nor were they in good enough condition to do anything with. I always believed that the cylinder head was the main reason that "Dutch's" little Chevy was so fast that day.

In 1918, when I was twelve years old, my father, in one of his frequent deals, acquired an old Model "T" Ford truck that began life as a touring car. The back half of the body had been removed and a "Smith Attachment" added. This consisted of another rear axle, two wheels, two frame rail extensions, two chains, four sprockets, another spring and two four-inch solid rubber tires, plus a sack full of nuts and bolts. To all of this, a flat bed from materials obtained locally, was added. It was supposed to be rated at one ton. I'd say it was more like a half-ton and just barely got by as a truck. The main idea was to get the gearing down low to increase pulling power and as a result, the top speed was cut way back. The original rear wheels were removed and replaced by two small sprockets. The two sprockets and wheel hubs went on the new solid axle and were driven by the two chains. The differential function was still provided by the original rear end. The new solid axle was stationary. The new hubs rotated on it through ball bearings. The new cross spring was the suspension for the solid axle.

Along with this mongrel, dad got a route that brought milk to a creamery and cheese factory that had just started up. He was doing the driving and I went along to help him. There was no starter on the truck, so I got to be the number one man on the crank. About this time, a big flu epidemic hit and everybody in our family got sick except me. I didn't know how come it missed me; maybe I was too ornery! There was no help to be hired. World War I was still going on and everyone was either sick or helping those who were. What we had was an awful mess.

It was up to me to take over the milk route. I'd have to get up early in the morning, milk our four cows and put out feed and water for the family's chickens. While that was taking place, I had oil and water for the truck in cans heating on the stove. I'd have a quick breakfast, pour the heated oil and water into the truck, twist the crank until it finally started and be on my way. The route was about fifty miles long and most of the farmers along the way treated me pretty good. They'd help me get those ten gallon milk cans up on the truck bed. When it rained, the recessed tops of those cans would fill up with water. When I'd swing the can up, the cold water would come out, splash in my face and run down the back of my neck. That sure kept me awake! I had a slow-moving truck and was always in a hurry, so I didn't want to take time to get the water out first. The guys in the creamery were good too. They'd help me unload the full cans and put on the next day's supply of empties.

A fellow named Art Prickett ran the milk route next to ours. He had a Reo truck that ran along pretty good, but he wasn't hauling as much weight as I was. He came up with the proposition that we combine the two routes and I help him on the Reo. We did this for a short time and then Art, who also had other things going, had to leave. He put another young fellow on to help me, because I knew the routes. This went on for some time until a neighbor of ours, who had been wounded in the war, came home and took over the milk routes. I was out of that job with no regrets.

Art Prickett started the American Transfer Company, which grew to be a large trucking operation in the San Joaquin Valley. I stopped in to visit him years later and we had quite a session reminiscing about those days.

There was a junkyard in town run by a man named Levy. He and my father were acquainted and Levy would let me in to look around and admire his fascinating collection. One of the things that kind of got me stirred up were some of the old motorcycles. I wanted to buy several of them, but that's hard to do without any money. So I made a deal with Levy to go in there on my spare time, Saturdays and Sundays, and help him sort metal. I got to know "yellow brass" from "red brass" from "copper." I worked quite religiously and slowly began to acquire old motorcycles and parts. I'd get them home to "monkey wrench" and play around with them. Eventually, I had thirteen of them and my mother reached the limit of her endurance. I was given the ultimatum to get rid of them, so my brother and I took them out and "hid" them behind the barn. We thought she didn't know where they were, but it was probably more of "out of sight, out of mind." Mothers are very special people.

One of our neighbors, a fellow named McClung, worked for the gas company and he was quite a good mechanic. He got home from work about four in the afternoon. Occasionally he would stop at our place and see what my brother and I were up to with these motorcycles. He never took his hands out of his pockets, but just talking to us he was a lot of help. We leaned on him for advice and information quite a bit. He never touched a tool or anything else, but told us how to go about finding and fixing what was wrong.

One of the motorcycles was a Cleveland. It had a two cycle

engine which we knew absolutely nothing about. So, in our innocence, we filled it up with oil and gas just like we would any other engine. I can't tell you exactly how, but we did manage to get motor oil down into the crankcase, where we found out later it wasn't supposed to be. We couldn't get it running, no matter how long or hard we tried. We flagged McClung down on his way home one afternoon and asked for help. He took one look at it and said, "Uh-oh!, did you boys put motor oil in the crankcase?" Yes, we had taken care of that. He told us to drain it all out and then proceeded to tell us all that we needed to know about two cycle engines. He explained to us that in a two cycle engine, the oil is mixed right in with the gas in a certain proportion, and provides lubrication as the incoming charge passes through the crankcase on its way to the combustion chamber; sort of a "throw away" oiling system. The spark plug had to be removed and cleaned of all that excess motor oil. By golly, once we had done all that he told us to do, it started right up. It smoked quite a bit, but he put us at ease by explaining that this was normal for a two cycle engine. We gained a lot of understanding from our good neighbor McClung and it wasn't forgotten. Years later, when I was getting into small time racing, he came down from the grandstand and into the pits to tell me I was doing real good. His words really meant a lot to me, and I never forgot them.

Getting Started

Wesley Edwards on the left and Herk Edwards on the right with two friends.

Herk's father, Walter, with "Eddie Gear" when a horse was almost a member of the family.   (Edwards Collection)

The Racing Bug Bites

Eventually, my dad got out of the real estate business and took a position with the J.B. Hill Company. They were in the grain and feed business and my father took over the feed department. At about the same time he took that job, we went into the chicken business at home. I imagine the two events were related. We had about fifteen hundred chickens on the ranch and my brother and I became the manpower pool to keep that operation going. We sure didn't care much for that. Whenever we wanted to go hunting, fishing or whatever, those chickens got in the way. They had to be fed and watered, eggs gathered and the chicken house cleaned. Life with those chickens was very dismal at times. Now, every time I eat chicken, I think about that flock of fifteen hundred chickens we had at home! Once my brother Wesley and I were no longer living with our parents, we made a solemn vow that neither of us, for our entire lives, would ever own a chicken. That vow was never broken!

My father bought a new 1919 Maxwell touring car to take him around the countryside in his new job. I'd already learned to handle the Model "T" by driving it around in the yard. I was soon driving my mother up to the edge of town and waiting for her there. She'd walk the several blocks to where her errands took her and then return to where I waited for the ride home. After awhile, I became brave enough to take her all the way into town and wait for her at her destination. Looking back, I'd say I was probably as good a driver as any of the others. At least, there were a lot of us starting out together.

One day, our beloved speed cop got into the picture. He had a Dodge with a speedster body on it. It was fixed up to where it was supposed to look fast, but I don't think Bill ever raced it. I doubt he ever caught anybody going over ten miles per hour. Bill could have been a Norman Rockwell original, a typical small-town speed cop. He had a leather cap, leather leggings, fancy riding breeches and a cigar. He liked to hang around the small garage and service station on the edge of town, posing and sort of putting himself on display. My dad knew him quite well.

One day, my dad and I stopped there to buy gas and dad struck up a conversation with him. My dad said, "Bill, what about this kid of mine getting a drivers license?" They were beginning to get a little sticky about things like that. Bill took off his leather cap, paused thoughtfully while scratching his head and said, "Well, I've been watching this kid drive and he's doing better than most of them. If he can answer a few questions for me, we'll see." So, he asked me about the rule of who has the "right of way," what the speed limits were and a number of things of that sort. I had all the answers and Bill Auberry gave a drivers license to an oversized fourteen-year-old-kid who still remembers it as a big day in his young life.

Dad's Maxwell was a gear shift car and I learned to manage that by driving it around in our yard. He wouldn't allow me to take that car into town.

Prior to the the 1920 Fresno County Fair, the construction of the one-mile board track was in progress while work on some of the exhibit buildings was also taking place. My father was in charge of maintenance and repairs for stock and poultry exhibits and had free access to the grounds. He hired a couple of guys to do the work and I was included in that crew. Once in awhile, I'd sneak over to the track and see how it was coming along. Boy, I tell you, when it was done it was a B-E-A-U-T-I-F-U-L thing! The first cars that showed were three Duesenbergs shipped to

Fresno in a baggage car and an Essex that was owned by Earl Palmer from nearby Sanger. My dad and I were there watching them try out the track. They looked great and the castor-oil lubricant they were using had a most delightful aroma as it fumed out of those roaring open exhaust pipes. I was completely caught up in the whole thing. My dad got to talking to one of the Duesenberg drivers. Wade Morton was a most congenial man and my dad asked him, "How about taking this kid of mine for a ride? He's always fooling around with cars and motors. Take him out there and scare the 'hell' out of him." Morton agreed, but said that my dad would have to sign a release and he could get that from the pit steward. My dad signed the waiver, came back to the car and had a few more words with Morton. Wade Morton put a spare leather helmet and a pair of goggles on me and I jumped right into that Duesenberg. We went out and ran a few laps and I tell you, oh boy, that was something else! I'm afraid it had exactly the wrong effect on me. From that moment on, I was totally hooked on racing. I don't think that was what my dad had in mind.

I returned to the track on my bicycle to see the race and I saw a good one. Morton had trouble that kept him out of the show. He would have been my favorite. How could it have been otherwise after my ride with him? Later, Wade Morton ran the Duesenbergs in the 1925 and 1927 Indy races. He was relieved in each race and both times the cars failed to finish; one crashed and one caught fire. Eventually, I lost track of Wade and don't know whatever became of him.

Anyhow, I was sure having a good time imagining myself out there as a driver or riding mechanic in one of the lead cars. Eddie O'Donnell started from the pole with Jimmy Murphy next in the pecking order. Positions got resorted during the 200 laps. Murphy came home the winner followed by O'Donnell, Tommy Milton and Gaston Chevrolet, who had won the Indy 500 in May and was the National Point Leader at the time.

Gaston had two brothers, Art and Louis Chevrolet. It was

Louis, the oldest, who had been an outstanding race driver for Buick (General Motors) and a creative thinker in things automotive. Louis made the mistake of getting tangled up with William C. (Crapo) Durant who was heading up the young General Motors Corporation. When Durant and Chevrolet parted company with bad feelings all around, Louis found out Durant and his legal eagles had managed to contractually deprive Chevrolet of the commercial use of his own last name. Louis chose "Frontenac" to identify the race cars he built and the after market line of Model "T" performance parts he and his brothers manufactured. Art was the production boss of the parts effort.

I was still hanging around the pits long after the race was over and just about everyone else was gone. Eddie O'Donnell and his mechanic were still there switching wheels and tires on the race car. The tires they were going to use to drive back into town were somewhat low in pressure. He asked me if I wanted to help and I got on that old hand pump and went to work without being asked a second time. They were skinny high pressure tires and I had a real workout. When everything was set, he asked me if I wanted to ride back into town with him. I said, "Sure," and hopped right in. It was only going to be a mile or so. That was the way they used to get the cars back and forth. I rode with him until he got to the downtown garage where they were keeping the car and then I walked back to the fairgrounds to get my bicycle and go home. That was another impressionable event in my young life that I never forgot, and it seemed to have a considerable impact on the way the years ahead unfolded.

After leaving Fresno, both Eddie O'Donnell and Gaston Chevrolet ran the November 1920 race on the Beverly Hills Board Speedway. Both bought the farm in the same pile-up late in the proceedings. O'Donnell's mechanic, Lyall Jolls, was also killed. Roscoe Sarles, who had also just run at Fresno, was included in the bad wreck at Beverly Hills. He survived that wreck only to be done in by a flaming crash at Kansas City in 1922.

The Racing Bug Bites

Dad eventually gave me the old Model "T" Ford. By that time, he had taken off the original body and made what might be called a pick-up out of it. He'd gotten hold of a very fancy leather upholstered seat out of a Pierce Arrow, I think it was. My dad had a little shop at home and he was quite good at working with wood. He built a cab for it and was able to haul a little hay as well as grain for those 'damned' chickens! I drove it back and forth to school. In bad weather, I'd give some of the neighbor kids a ride. One morning, as I was getting ready to leave for school, I saw I had a flat tire. The neighbor girl, who was something of a "tomboy," was going to ride with me; so she just stepped in and helped me with the whole operation—patch the tube and the whole bit. She was way ahead of her time.

After awhile, this old Ford had become awfully tired. It got to where I had to crank it so hard and long, that it just about wore me out. It was becoming almost impossible to start. Dad was acquainted with Tom Newton, a mechanic who ran a little garage in town. Tom told dad that those old Fords tended to wear off the thrust bearing on the back of the crankshaft and that made too much gap for the magnets on the flywheel to do their job of energizing the coils. He told us the way to fix that was to take the engine all apart and build that bearing flange up with solder. Then we should take a file or bearing scraper and bring it back down to the correct thickness. We would then get the proper amount of spark need to start the engine.

By this time, I was in high school taking an auto shop class along with my other subjects. We were doing minor work on the school buses such as tune-ups and things like that. I told my instructor about the problem with the Ford and asked if I could bring it in and work on it there. He said that I could, so I got it started one more time, brought it in and went to work on it. I did this for about an hour a day during class. The shop had a chain hoist and all the hand tools I needed. With the help of several other kids, I had the engine out and on the floor in no time at all. Remembering the garage man's instructions, I got out the

25

soldering equipment and made the repair. The instructor seemed unfamiliar with what I was doing so he left me on my own. He then agreed to let me work on it after school too, so it wasn't long before I had it all back together and running. After that, a few twists of the crank and it would start right up.

I could handle the shop class in high school O.K., but the academic side and all the rest left me with a strong desire to be in another place. I had a lot of other things on my mind besides my lessons. The old Model "T" gave me a sense of freedom and maturity that few kids in my high school had. I wanted out! The chicken business at home was also getting to me. I had to get up early and go through all that ritual, then come home and have to go through it all over again.

A fellow in school named Hugh Withrow had been telling me about a logging camp up in the mountains around Huntington Lake, or Big Creek as they called it back then. He was going up there to get a job. He didn't tell me, but I found out later that his older sister Leslie was married to Sam Kelner, the owner of the mill up there. He had a connection and I didn't, but it made no difference. I filled the old Ford with gas and went up there, got to see the boss and told him I wanted a job; it was almost noon. He asked me if I had ever worked around the woods before. I told him I hadn't, but my dad had. Well, he didn't know if that was going to help me very much. He paused for a moment and then told me to go over where the men were having lunch and get something to eat. While I was doing that, he'd call over to the Wood's Boss and see if there were any openings.

I did get a job firing one of the donkey engines and later I got to run it. I fit in there pretty well and felt good about what I was doing. I liked being around machinery. We had a couple of snow storms around Thanksgiving that sort of slowed things down. It wasn't long afterward that the camp had to be closed down for the rest of the year. They told me that if I wanted to come back the following year, I could have a job. That was good to know, but I had already decided I was going to try for something more steady.

The Racing Bug Bites

When I got home from logging camp, I had some money in my pocket so I moved up a little and bought a 1918 or '19 Nash roadster. My younger brother, Wesley, took over the Model "T" and ran it for awhile. He later traded it in on a Chevrolet roadster. I used to see the old Ford around town now and then until it kind of disappeared.

Now that I was home again, I decided to do something about my interrupted education and signed up for night school. I enrolled in the "Machine Shop" and "Auto Repair" classes, jumping back and forth between the two, depending on which was most interesting at the time.

Mr. Schuller, the automotive instructor was quite a guy. He had two old automobile engines set up on stands with radiators, gas lines, exhaust connections and the whole bit so they could be run. When he got us past the preliminaries and fundamentals, it became hands-on training.

He organized the class into teams of two boys on each team and then put them to work in that manner. He'd say, "Now you two boys take that Mercer engine and get it started. You two boys, there, do the same; get that Nordyke running." There were no self starters on those engines so we had to work hard hand-cranking them. He had a little office off to one side. At first, when we couldn't get our engine going, we'd go into his office and tell him so. Then he'd say, "Now look, boys, if it has spark at the proper moment and gasoline and compression, it will have to run." We'd scratch our heads and go back out to see what we could find. We might come back to him and say, "Mr. Schuller, we think it's got no spark." He'd reply, "Well boys, you don't 'think,' you either know or you don't know. How do you know? You pull off a spark plug wire and you check it. If it's got no spark, you find out why. If it has spark, then has it got gasoline? You can take out a spark plug to see. If it's wet and smells like gasoline, then it's getting gasoline. Is it in time? You check the timing. If that's right and everything else is right, it's going to run. You know it was made to run." He was right, of course.

The Bobby The Babe and Me

Mr. Schuller had to be the world's greatest fixer-upper, so far as putting trouble into an engine was concerned. He'd solder a gas line shut, short out the spark plug electrodes, use spark plug wires with no wire in them, jack a valve open with the tappet so it'd never close or set the points wrong in the magneto. He had a bag full of tricks, and after awhile we learned them all.

Whenever we discovered what he'd done to prevent our engine from running, we kept it to ourselves. When the next two fellows would be cranking and cranking, trying to get the engine started, we'd stand around and snicker. It didn't take us long to become experts and big shots; or so we thought. Mr. Schuller taught me in a way that made a lasting impression and was one of the best teachers I ever had. His teaching me my favorite subject may have given me an advantage.

As a result of my exposure to metal working machines in night school, I got a day job with Charley Sickler in his machine shop. At that time, automobile flywheels were made entirely out of cast iron and that included the teeth around the outer edge that meshed with the starter gear. With extended use, some of the flywheel teeth would wear out or break off causing trouble getting started. Some shops would screw in pins to replace the missing teeth or weld in new material to form replacing teeth. Neither of these two methods was a totally satisfactory repair. Fix it in one place and it would go bad in another. The Mann Manufacturing Company in Emoryville came up with the great idea of having a steel ring with teeth machined on it to make the repair. That became my job at Sickler's machine shop and he had a big old engine lathe for me to cut the teeth off those flywheels. Power to the lathe was through a Chevrolet transmission, which cut the spindle speed way down and put power at the cutting tool way up. That baby could really make chips! I'd cut on the flywheel to receive the new ring gear, checking carefully with a large caliper as I went along. Once I had it down to a specific measurement, the next step was to shrink on the ring gear. The new ring gear was heated over a gas flame to expand it, then placed on the newly machined surface of the old flywheel and allowed to cool. Once it had done that, it was there to stay and made the whole unit better than new. Charley picked up the old flywheels from junkyards and we had stacks of them sitting around. He became a source of rebuilt flywheels for Western Auto and other parts houses. Charley's was my first paying job using metal working machinery.

Charley seemed to be interested in "hop-up" and racing equipment and was agreeable to my bringing in motorcycles or automotive items to work on in my spare time or when shop work slacked off.

One of the things I managed to get hold of was a 16 valve Craig-Hunt head for a Model "T" Ford. This was a "single cam head," and in order to operate that complement of valves, the rocker arms were forked at the valve end and did double duty. The cam end was roller equipped. The camshaft was chain driven off of the crankshaft. Later on, I understand, the chain and sprockets were replaced with a vertical shaft and bevel gears. The whole set-up was much like Mercedes used on the 1915 Indy winner with Ralph DePalma driving. Those early Mercedes engines were designed for World War I aircraft and just brought down to earth and put on wheels for auto racing. I don't recall where I got it, but it sure would be a nice thing to have now. One of the bolt holes for holding a cam bearing in place was stripped. Charley showed me how to repair the bad hole. We tapped it out to a slightly larger size and turned up a threaded sleeve with matching threads on the O.D. and the original thread size on the I.D. That worked real good. The camshaft was shot, but the lobes were O.K. and being pinned on, I was able to get them off. I tooled up another shaft and Charley picked up another Ford as a spare car. I put that cylinder head on it and that really made it go. I only had it for a short while, when a fellow who worked at a nearby service station began pestering me for it. I sold him the cylinder head for $15.00 and was sorry ever since. I found out later the complete head with all the pieces sold for $85.00. I wasn't earning that much money in a month; or maybe two.

I saw the guy later on and asked him how he was making out with it. He said he'd been street racing with some other fellow and wound up breaking an axle shaft. He decided to let the car go and not fool around with it anymore. I lost track of it and later found out I had owned a very rare cylinder head; one of a very few like it that had ever been built for a Model "T" Ford.

Charley was quite a guy to go out and drum up work for his shop. When the flywheel business began to slow down, he got in with Myers Pump of Fresno and picked up some of their work. They weren't able to handle all of it themselves, so we got to do some machining on their centrifugal pump castings.

One of the kids I got acquainted with at night school was Oliver Clough. He later became quite well known as a motor-cycle hill climber. He was doing work for Charley Sickler, too, along with another fellow named Dick King. We called him "Racer" Dick, because that's all he ever wanted to talk about. We figured he deserved that nickname and it didn't seem to bother him. He might even have liked it and didn't want to let on for fear we might stop calling him that. So, Charley had three young kids helping him who were all interested in racing. Charley had been known to take a drink on occasion and they weren't all national holidays! When he took off to go down to his favorite bootlegger to get a snoot full, the three of us were left in the shop alone. That's when we got to doing other things besides machining flywheels or centrifugal pump castings. We decided to build a rotary valve set-up for an old nameless English motorcycle engine that was laying around the shop.

When Charley would leave, one of us would stay at the front door and the other two would be playing around with the rotary valve project. At a signal from the lookout, everything would go back under the bench into a special hiding place we had. We'd hurry back to doing what it was we were supposed to be doing.

One of our favorite hangouts was the local Harley-Davidson shop, where they also sold an English motorcycle magazine.

The Racing Bug Bites

One day, "Racer" Dick came to work with one of those magazines and he looked very dejected. He showed us a picture of a rotary valve that was being made over there and it was just about the same as we'd been trying to do. That picture put an end to our project. No use in trying to reinvent the light bulb!

Young Meyers, son of the pump company owner, got together with Charley and made a deal. All of a sudden there were all these pump castings coming in for machining and they didn't have the "Meyers" name cast on them. We went on working with these for quite awhile and Charley had us keep these separate and pile the ones we'd finished with out in the back. One day, out of the blue, old man Meyers came into the shop and began looking around at everything. When he found those nameless pump castings, finished and unfinished, he really blew up.

Come to find out, young Meyers was taking his father's pump patterns over to another foundry in Fresno and having them cast there. Charley was machining them and young Meyers was selling them on the side at quite a discount! That was the end of "free enterprise" within the Meyers family, along with the sudden drying up of the pump machining work for Charley Sickler.

Charley wasn't doing much in his shop after that and I had to find another job. He never paid us very much, but then, I don't think he ever made very much from our work either.

Wade Morton
(McNamara Collection)

Eddie O'Donnell   (Fabritz Collection)

31

Herk Edwards' first wheels. The once new Ford Touring Car
modified for more utilitarian service. (Edwards Collection)

Herk with his second car, a Nash, acquired after logging camp vastly improved his net worth.

(Edwards Collection)

Reaching Out

After I left Charlie Sickler, I got a temporary job putting out promotional material for "Black and White" brand shoe polish. Another fellow and I traveled around a good bit placing postcards and signs in shoe stores and shoe repair shops.

On one of our first trips down to Los Angeles, about 1925-26, we had some free time on a Saturday. I'd heard that there was usually somebody out at Ascot Speedway fiddling around with a race car, so we went over there. A fellow named Cliff Wilson was at the track with a brand new, well-made, nice-looking Chevy-powered race car. One of the guys standing there told me Wilson had owned an older car, but after coming into some money he'd built this new one. They towed the car to get it started and it'd go "SPUT SPUT, BANG BANG, POP POP" and never get going. They'd bring it in, check it over, fool around, take it out and try it again; same thing! I watched these goings on from the stands for awhile and it got me interested. After he'd gone through that fire drill three or four times, I couldn't stand it any more, so I got up and walked over to the group around the car. I just stood there looking over some shoulders.

Being familiar with Chevrolet, I knew that the generator which was on the right-hand side of the engine, had a shaft that ran right straight through. It was driven from the forward end and the other end went into a little right-angled gear box that rotated the distributor. The ratio in the gear box was something other than one to one, because of a need to compensate for the ratio at which the generator shaft was being turned relative to the engine. When these two ratios, input and output, were figured together, the result was that the distributor would make one revolution while the engine made two.When you wanted to replace the distributor and generator with a magneto, for racing purposes, one of the options was to use the set-up for the front of the engine that came with the old Samson truck. There weren't many of these old trucks still laying around, so most guys worked out their own little details to drive the magneto. Some gutted the generator, left it on the engine and drove the magneto off of the back end. Of course, they still had to get involved with some gearing to take care of that ratio problem.

I was just a nineteen-year-old punk kid, standing around watching these race car experts try to get a new car going. They had pulled the magneto off and were looking at it for the answer. Cliff Wilson's car had the magneto running directly off the timing gears behind the front cover. The magneto was held in position with a little bracketing arrangement they had worked out. I was thinking about their problem, too, and when the light went on, I blurted out, "Mr. Wilson, did you put a Samson front end on your engine? How did you get the gears to compensate for the angle drive?" He turned towards me with a vacant look on his face. Suddenly, his eyes lit up and his hair seemed to stand on end. He started cussing and throwing tools around, and I thought, Oh boy! I've really done it now! He walked around in a circle two or three times before he could get out the words, "I'll be goll-darned, I'll be G-O-L-L- Darned! I've worked on this car for two years and I knew all about that gear ratio difference and I never did a thing about it. Of all the stupid things _____." He went on that way for quite awhile and I figured I'd made him mad, so I backed up a bit. A little while later, one of the fellows that was with him came over and assured me that his little demonstration wasn't directed at me. He was just mad at himself. They bundled up the car and took it home.

Reaching Out

The next time I saw the car, it was up at San Jose and it was running good. So I went over and asked him how things were going and if he remembered me. He paused for a moment, looked me over and said, "Yah! I do, you're that kid that told me what was the matter with my car down at Ascot." He laughed about it and said, "You know, I've done a lot of dumb things in my time, but that was about the dumbest thing I ever did."

One of the other young fellows looking on that day at Ascot was also a Chevrolet man. We both had more than a passing interest in Cliff Wilson's Chevy, so we struck up a conversation. He told me he was building a Chevy in a shop he'd rented out in Venice. We traded opinions, ideas and information back and forth. He told me his name was Perry Bertrand, and if I got a chance, to come out and have a look at his race car. A day or so later, I went to see him at his shop. The car was coming along and I liked what I saw. He said that if I wasn't doing anything that evening, to stick around and give him a hand. I got so involved that I wound up staying with him for three days helping with the car. We had a lot of fun working on it together and became very well acquainted. He was a nice guy to be around. Bertrand was a "racer" too and eventually became well known as a cam grinder.

Quite a few years later, I needed a cam for the Keim midget and called Bertrand. I told him who was calling and he said, "Oh yes, I remember you." We reminisced about our earlier association before getting down to business at hand. So he got to grind the cam for the Keim and did a quality job of it.

On that same early trip down to Los Angeles, I went out to Ascot to see the races. I got myself down into the pits, somehow, to be close to the action. I knew Bill Bundy, who was there that day with an old Fronty, so I got to hang around his pit. This was an outlaw race and that brought out a bunch of junkers. Of all the cars that were out there, only one stood out from all the others. It was quite a beautiful thing. All of a sudden, I saw the driver who'd been in the car hurrying over in our direction. I heard him ask Bill if he could hide in his pit. There was no problem with that, so he hunkered down and we threw a canvas car cover over him. Bill motioned to me to keep my mouth shut. Not much later, along comes this nicely-dressed gentleman, giving the definite impression that he's looking for something or somebody. He asked Bill, "Have you seen the driver of that car parked over there?" and he pointed to the pretty one.

"Yup," says Bill, "he went past here a little bit ago—heading for the toilets, I'd guess."

"Do you know who it was?"

"No!" says Bill, "I never saw him before."

After the gentleman left, Bill told me, "That was Art Pillsbury, the Regional AAA Representative, looking for the guy under the tarp."

Our shy recluse was AAA driver, Bon McDougal, who had in mind to run the non-sanctioned event under another name. If he got caught doing such a dastardly thing, AAA would hit him with a fine, suspension or something else he didn't really want. I didn't know much about AAA, in those days, but I was beginning to learn. McDougal stuck his head out from under the cover and wanted to know if Pillsbury was gone. "No, he isn't, and you better stay where you are for awhile," said Bill. We kept an eye on Pillsbury as he moved around, and when he got far enough away from us, we told McDougal his moment had arrived. When he came out from under the canvas, he hurried off in the opposite direction. The risk of running into Pillsbury was too great, so McDougal removed himself from the track without further delay. Someone else drove the handsome little car to a win that day. I don't know who it was, but I thought, "What a lucky guy!"

While growing up in Fresno, we had good solid neighbors in the Lemke family. The parents had come over from Germany and were fine people. Of course, we kids got to know their two sons, Reuben and Irvin. When I finished the "Black and White" advertising promotion, I went to work in the shop of the Appling and Rodman Chevrolet dealership in Fresno. Rube Lemke was already working there and had been for some time. He stayed with them for many years and got to be their shop foreman. He eventually left them to start up his own auto repair business.

One of my first jobs at Appling and Rodman was to go down to the railroad yard and help bring back the new automobiles. They shipped them in box cars, standing somewhat up on end. We maneuvered them out, towed them back and got them ready to sell. I guess now they would call that "Dealer Prep." We'd check the brakes, set the valve clearance, put in the oil and water, and generally get them ready to roll.

The shop foreman, George Miller, Rube Lemke and I were all interested in hopping up the Chevrolet automobile and this we did in our spare time. We usually went the cylinder head route in our search for more performance. We'd go to the wrecking yards looking for three port heads off the Chevrolet "Baby Grand," Oldsmobile or Samson truck. We'd put in the larger Fordson tractor valves after shortening the stems and making new keeper grooves. We used Essex valve springs which were stiffer and would allow the engine to turn faster without the valves "floating." We had a lot of fun doing that and the results were gratifying.

Another young fellow around Fresno then, who also enjoyed doing that sort of thing, was Fred Gerhardt. His dad had a ranch a little way out of town. Rube and I would go out there to swap engines. They had a big apricot tree with a block and tackle hanging in it, just the thing for changing engines. Fred Gerhardt became a well known race car owner and had cars at Indianapolis in the fifties and sixties. He and I got together in his race shop years later, and laughed about the things we'd done in earlier times.

After I left Appling and Rodman, George Miller built a four-cylinder race car that he called the Fresno Special. He worked on it at odd times and so did Rube Lemke and some of the other guys around the shop, kind of a group project. George, being shop foreman, was able to direct their efforts as opportunities to work on the car arose. As it turned out, it was never very much for speed, so it was available to any number of drivers. Kelly Petillo drove it, Al Chasteen drove it, I drove it, and so did a bunch of other guys. George never came up with a regular driver, so he'd go to the track and pick up some guy without a car. A lot of fellows had their first ride in the Fresno Special.

Things began to slow down at the Appling and Rodman garage. We had changed over to working "flat rate" and there wasn't enough work coming in to keep some of us from sitting around. One morning, George Miller came out of his office and told us that he'd just had a call from Art Dahlsheim over in Coalinga, and he was looking for help. Coalinga lay about fifty miles south and west of Fresno, as the crow flies. Art had the Chevrolet agency over there along with a machine shop. He was paying fifty-five cents an hour and had lots of work. That seemed to suit me just fine. When the other guys didn't say anything and just looked around at each other, I said, "By golly, I'll go!" George said "O.K., you call him up and make the deal." I got Dahlsheim on the phone; he told me he needed someone soon and asked when I was coming over. I told him, "Right now!" He said rooms were kind of hard to get, but he thought he could find a place for me to stay that night, so I should come right away.

I proceeded to load up my tools in my 1923 four-cylinder Chevy, went home, put some clothes in a suitcase and I was on my way to Coalinga. I only got part way out of Fresno and the Chevy quit on me. It had a cone clutch and that's what gave up the ghost. There was a friend living nearby who came to my rescue. We transferred my belongings to his car and he and his wife drove me over there. By the time we arrived at Dahlsheim's garage, the only person on the premises was the evening man who was handling the gas pumps. I told him about my coming to work for Dahlsheim and that there was supposed to be a place arranged for me to stay the night. Well, he didn't know beans about it; nobody had told him anything. I imagine when I was a little late showing up, they decided I wasn't coming. Not having any other place to put my tools and suitcase, I left them at the garage. My friend, his wife and I found a restaurant and had something to eat. Then, we went around looking for a place for me to stay and we came up with nothing. It was about time that my friend and his wife should be returning to Fresno, so they dropped me off at the garage. I thanked them for all their help before they took off, and I turned in at the "Dahlsheim Hilton." I crawled into the back of one of the cars and spent a quiet night there.

When Mr. Dahlsheim came in the following morning, we went over to Ma Watton's place. This was a big old three-story mansion, that belonged to one of the original oil barons in Coalinga. It didn't look like a rooming house, and that was the reason we hadn't checked it out the night before. It was in the center of town and took up about half a city block. Ma had taken the first floor and made a kitchen and dining room out of it. The two upper floors were sleeping rooms that she rented out. I'll tell you, she sure put out some great meals. At noontime, she drew traveling salesmen, tradesmen, shop owners, professional people, and anybody else who liked to eat. It was all served family-style at a big long table and you had to get there ahead of time to be sure of having a place. She had three or four local girls helping serve and clean up. I stayed and ate there, and still have fond memories of her place.

Business at Dahlsheim's Chevrolet dealership was going great and I was working ten to twelve hours a day. At fifty-five cents an hour and with all those hours, I was making more money than I ever had. I fit in quite well at Dahlsheim's doing both auto repair and machine shop work for him. My experience at both may have been one of the reasons I got the job.

A foreman would come into the machine shop from a large company called Lange Excavation. They were headquartered in the Los Angeles area, and one of the pieces of equipment they operated was a large ditch digger. The problem they were having with it had to do with the short life of the pivot pins, of which there were many. The replacements we were making for them didn't last very long either. The down time needed to change pins was something that bothered them too.

I'd put in a full day at the garage and then come back after supper to work overtime in the machine shop making up those big one-inch pins. One time, we'd run out of one-inch stock and I thought of making them out of old Ford rear axle shafts which were the same diameter. If the rear hubs weren't kept snug, the key ways in the axle shafts would wear out and you could pick the old ones up for junk. I got hold of a bunch of those, cut them into four-inch lengths on the power saw and tooled them into finished pins. When finished, they looked just the same as the ones I had been making. I gave this new batch of pins to the foreman and told him what I'd made them from. After that he didn't come in for new pins nearly as often. Art Dahlsheim didn't seem to catch on to what was taking place; he was probably too busy with other things.

One evening, while I was busy in the machine shop with other work, a big red chauffeur-driven Lincoln touring car pulled up in front of the place with the foreman and another fellow seated in the back. They came over and the foreman said to the other gentleman, "This is the guy I've been telling you about." So, I met Mike Lange, the multi-millionaire head of the company that bore his name. He had come over from Ireland as a young man, and began digging ditches with a pick and shovel. He'd come a long way, and he did it on his own.

"Herk," he said, "You're a pretty smart kid and you sure saved us a bundle on those pins." We had a "chit-chat" back and forth and he asked me if I ever took a drink. "Oh, once in a while," I told him. He walked over to the Lincoln and came back with a gallon of whiskey. He gave me a drink and it was pretty good stuff! "By the way, kid, if you ever want a job, come on down and just ask for Mike Lange. Here's a little present for you," and he handed me the gallon jug of whiskey.

Reaching Out

While I was working for Dahlsheim in Coalinga, my good friend Rube found out about a beautiful little Chevy race car that could be had for $350.00. He wanted me to come in as partner on it and I liked that idea. It had a very nice hand-built body and radiator shell. The big oil pan was special and would hold about five gallons. The fellow that owned and drove the car was Freddie Lyons from Los Angeles. He was a sort of a "Ham and Egger," running in races with the big guys and just getting by. Going through the fence at Reno, Nevada, put him in the hospital for quite awhile. After that, he ran a few more races, but didn't do very well at all. He came up to Fresno for a race and went broke in the process. That's how Rube and I came to own the car. Freddie was a great talker and always claimed that he and Frank Lockhart were great buddies, but when I'd see both of them at the same track, they never seemed to be together. I did hear of the time that Lyons was having trouble with his car at the track. He tipped it up on two wheels and took off the oil pan. He suspected a bearing problem and when he got the crankshaft exposed, he wanted to measure it. He went over to his "friend," Frank Lockhart, and asked to borrow a mike (micrometer). Frank asked what he wanted to do with it and Freddie told him. Lockhart's reply was said to have been, "Guess at it! You've been guessing at everything else."

Whenever I could get free on a weekend, I'd run back to Fresno and Rube and I would take the race car out to the half-mile track at the Fresno County Fairgrounds. The dilapidated old board track was still standing and the new half-mile had been built inside of it. It was used primarily to exercise the trotting horses that were stabled at the grounds. Freddie Lyons stopped by one day when we were out there. He took the car out for several laps to show us how to get it around. Then Rube and I each took turns running it round and round, seeing how good we could do and pretending we were real race drivers. We sure had a good time doing that. Freddie Lyons stayed around Fresno for a little while and then moved up to San Jose. He got into a few races there, but didn't do a whole lot.

Rube Lemke's mother got wind of these goings on and took a dim view of the whole thing. She had, no doubt, heard of race drivers getting killed and got on Rube about it. Anyhow, Rube decided to sell me his share of the car, so I became sole owner and took it back to Coalinga with me. Rube never did get to actually race the Chevy while we were together on it; he just fooled around. The new four-cylinder Chevy model had just come out, and being a Chevy man, I looked at that new two port cylinder head and began to see possibilities.

It got so that I was spending more time on the Chevy race car at Dahlsheim's than Art Dahlsheim thought I should, so we came to a parting of the ways.

There was a Buick garage in Coalinga run by a fellow named Harold Hawley, who I'd heard was building a four-cylinder Buick race car. I went over there to see what he was up to. Well, he gave me a big song and dance about all the race car drivers and owners that he knew and the rest of that kind of smoke. He was really laying it on, and while I wasn't saying anything, I wasn't buying all of it either. We did have a common interest and that was what led me to go to work for him.

We'd go down to the shop to work on his race car. The chassis was nearing completion and he'd done a nice job on it. We were getting along real well, and at one point, he decided he was not going to put his Buick engine in the car. His idea was to take the engine out of my race car and put it into his. I don't recall how he convinced me to do that, but it became the direction in which we were going. It was at this time that we heard of a race coming up at Chowchilla. Neither of our cars were able to run, but we decided to go up and see the show. We got into the pits, looked at the cars close up, and watched the racing from there. The little *"Bobby Special"* was at the track that day, and it just ran off and hid from everybody. A fellow named Ray Walters was driving it, and that was the only time he got to drive it. Later the story went around that Walters wound up in San Quentin on a bad check rap and, of course, there wasn't much auto racing going on up there! I got to talk to Charley Bobby, the builder and owner of the car, and he seemed interested in what I was doing. I told him of my working in the Buick garage, the race cars and all of that. He told me about his shop in Watsonville, how busy he was and if I wanted a job to come on up.

On the way back to Coalinga, I decided to make the move to Watsonville. I wanted to take my engine out of Harold Hawley's race car and put it back into mine, but he didn't see it quite that way. He got a shyster lawyer friend of his involved and took custody of my personal property through legal attachment. It got to be a big "hoop-te-do" and I left for Watsonville without my race car or engine. Later on, I got a letter from Harold Hawley saying that it wasn't right for him to keep my engine, and if I wanted, I could come down and get it.

I drove to Coalinga in an old four-cylinder Chevy touring car. I put the race car engine in the back of it and flat-towed the rest of it. I got everything back to Watsonville O.K., and that was the end of that caper. I saw Harold Hawley again a number of years later. We were racing midgets at Fresno one night, when he came down to the pits to say hello. He was then a foreman for the Caterpillar Tractor Company in Modesto, California. He said that he never finished the Buick race car and left it in Coalinga when he moved away. He didn't know what ever became of it.

Ray Walters in the Bobby poses with promoter, Linn Mathewson in 1927.

Freddie Lyon's zero cash balance gave Herk Edwards the chance to own this race car.

Herk Edwards, the fledging race car pilot and George Miller, the proud owner of the 490 Chevrolet.

Babe and the Bobby

Charley Bobby had a Nash agency in Watsonville, California, with a shop full of work and a little eight-valve Fronty Ford racing car. Charley was of English heritage, an excellent mechanic, and a man who sought perfection above all else. For Charley, things were either right or wrong, with nothing in between being acceptable. Of course I was very drawn to the race car and got to work on it under Charley's supervision. A fellow named Jack Buxton was Charley's driver. He was a big, tall man of impressive, perhaps regal, bearing that got him the nickname "Lord" Buxton. He was also a sports writer and had considerable artistic talents. He did sketches of race car subjects that were very good. We'd see him around the shop frequently. He drove the car at San Jose a number of times and did quite well. Toward the end of 1927, a bunch of guys gathered at Fresno for an outlaw race that was being put on by a fellow named DeBolt. He didn't have much of a crew to handle the event, but Eddie Meyer, Louie Meyer's older brother, was there to work the flags.

The old one-mile board track was still in place at the Fresno County Fairgrounds, but in sad shape, no longer fit for even short races. A new half-mile dirt track had been built in the infield, and this was to be the first race on it.

About fourteen cars showed up with Lou Moore, Ernie Triplett, Bill Spence, Barney Kloepfer, Mel Kenealy and other west coast hot shoes to do the chauffeuring. Jack Buxton and the

Bobby Special were there too. Jack wore a turtleneck with *"Bobby Spl."* lettered across the chest. Even when he wasn't in or around his car at the track, you knew which car he was driving. Jack and Charley were proud people, and it was reflected in how they presented themselves and the car to the public.

The program that day consisted of three 5-mile preliminary heat races, a 10-mile consolation race and a 25-mile feature. Buxton came in second behind Barney Kloepfer in their preliminary, and Lou Moore took the 50-lap feature with Kloepfer second and Buxton following for third. That third was arrived at only after the "Bobby" crew raised hell with the officials about being given fourth behind Bill Spence. The official records were of no value or nonexistent. Only after getting help from notes that sports reporters had made during the race was justice done. Bill Spence was ahead of Buxton on the track but a lap down and was given fourth.

Eight cars had started the race and six finished. Mel Kenealy went out when his car caught fire early in the race. Harry Jacques rolled his car about half way through and landed with his wheels in the air. He was able to wiggle out of the car without help and was none the worse for the experience.

In 1929, Jack Buxton went back to Indianapolis to drive the Lloyd Corliss Miller. I believe it was in practice that the hood got loose, came back, and tried to take his head off. That may have slowed him up a little. He did get to drive relief for Herman Schurch in the same car during the 500 Mile Race. It was the #31 Armacost Miller entered by Fred Schneider and owned by Lloyd Corliss. The gas tank split after seventy laps and the car was retired. His experience at Indianapolis seemed to take the wind out of his sails. Most everyone said he wasn't nearly as good a driver after Indy. Jack and Charley ended their special relationship soon after.

Charley had been down to Ascot Speedway and was impressed with the driving of a fellow named "Babe" Stapp. Babe had become one of the nation's top drivers in the few years since his first race on June 4, of 1923 at San Luis Obispo, where he drove George Sherman's Special. He and Charley worked out a deal in 1930 where Babe could go back to Indianapolis after the first of the year to work with the Duesenberg brothers, and then drive one of their cars in the 500. When Babe returned after the race, the Bobby car was his.

Babe would tell me stories about Indianapolis and some of the people that he'd met there while he and I worked on the car together. One of those people was Wilbur Shaw, and years later when Shaw's book "Gentlemen, Start Your Engines" came out, some of the passages were familiar. Wilbur had told things to Babe that were later included in the book, and Babe had related them to me. Babe was good with a story as well as in conversation. When Babe was back east, Mel Kenealy, Speed Hinckley or Carl Ryder would drive the car.

At odd times in Charley's shop, when I could squeeze it in, I'd try to do some work on my car and get it ready for a race. I had run in some races with AAA on temporary permits and felt it was time for me to go for a full AAA license. I had put my Chevy race car back together again in what spare time was available. This was the Chevy that Rube Lemke and I had owned jointly. One Sunday I took the car up to San Jose and talked to Frank Hood, the local AAA representative, about getting a license. He gave me my temporary permit for that day and told me I'd have to see Mr. Fred Wagner about taking a driver's test. Fred Wagner was the race starter and the man in charge on the scene for AAA. He was involved in racing from the beginning, crisscrossing the country from one end to the other, exercising his brand of authority that was firm, fair, and even-handed. He became a sort of father figure so it was natural that as the years piled on, he was thought of and referred to as "Pop" Wagner. I approached Mr. Wagner, showed him my permit and told him I was interested in getting a license. The first thing he asked was if I understood the meaning of the different colors of the flags. I told him I did and he said, "Well, let's find out!" So he had me tell him all about the flags. He said I had learned that lesson very well; next would be the driving test.

There were a few cars out on the track warming up, so he said, "You get your car out, put it on the line over there and wait for a few minutes. I'll let you know when to go out." After a bit the pit manager came over and told me, "Mr. Wagner said for you to go out." I got into my car and when I got the flag, I was on my way. I tore around there in that old Chevy with everything open but the tool box. I must have been doing all of sixty-five miles per hour. I kept on tearing around there as fast as I could until Pop Wagner flagged me in. I parked it in the pits and went over to ask him how I'd done. "Well, son," he said, "You did OK. You're a little shy on steam, but I think you'll make it all right." So I got my AAA license and I was very happy about that.

Later on, I was in Pop Wagner's presence a number of times and listened to him tell stories to whoever was gathered around. Wagner often told the story about Eddie Hearne involving a dirt track race at Reno, Nevada. Before the race, they'd had a stock show in front of the grandstand on the main stretch; all those horses and cows were parading back and forth. Seems like they left a lot of manure on the track and then started the race without cleaning any of it up. At one point during the race, Hearne was running right behind another car that threw a bunch of that up in the air and Hearne drove right into it. It hit him square in the face, so he came in to clean up and get fresh goggles. Wagner got hold of an old loving cup somewhere and filled it up with horse manure. He presented it to Eddie after the race and named him the Horse Manure Champion of Reno. That title stuck with Hearne for quite awhile. Pop Wagner was a wonderful story teller, who really held your attention and always left you wanting to hear more.

I was serious about this racing business and wanted to be more directly involved. Finally, Charley came over to me one day and said, "Why don't you just forget that old piece of junk and concentrate on the Bobby? When Babe goes back to Indianapolis, I'll let you drive it." Well, that sounded awfully good to me. I could hardly believe it, but I sure wanted to. So I got rid of my race car as part of the bargain, but Charley kind of forgot about his part when it came to be race time. I was there and available, but it was always another driver in the car. So once we got the Bobby all ready at the track, I'd get a ride in someone else's car. Charley didn't appear to like that very much, but he went along with it. The racing bug had bitten pretty good.

Ernie Ruiz of Modesto bought my Chevy race car. He later became famous with his Travelon Trailer entries in the 500 Mile Races of the fifties and sixties. What Ernie finally did with my old car remains a mystery.

I got acquainted with Gordon Webster when I was down at the El Centro race track with the Bobby. I had seen him around at San Jose too. At El Centro, he came over and asked me if I wanted to drive his car, an old rocker arm Fronty. He kind of talked it up a little, told me how good it was and all of that sort of thing. I asked Charley Bobby about my doing that and he said it would be alright as long as everything was under control in his pit. So I took Webster's car out on the track. It made a lot of racket out there, so I came in and told him about it. The engine was making a lot of clatter. He said not to worry about it. He'd put a new cam in it and one thing and another. "It makes a lot of noise. That's the way it is. Don't pay any attention to that. Just put your foot in it and it'll go." So when it came time for me to qualify the car, I went out and put my foot in it up to the ankle, I think! I took the flag, went down through the first turn and was heading down the back straight. All of a sudden the whole steering came loose and all hell broke loose in the cockpit down around my feet. I got them up out of that hole in a hurry! In that car, like a lot of others, the steering gear was mounted on top of the transmission cover. The flywheel had exploded and tore everything apart down there. I managed to get the car stopped on the track. The tow truck came out and brought me in. I went over to the ambulance and got my legs bandaged. That was all for Webster's Fronty for that day.

I asked him a few questions and found out why the thing blew up. Webster had taken a Model "A" flywheel, turned it down to lighten it and to work with the multi-disk clutch he had. What he hadn't done was to shrink a steel band onto the circumference to keep what was left of that cast iron flywheel from coming apart. Most everyone knew of that routine. Webster learned about it that day and I've got the scars on my shins to prove it.

Webster's cousin, Roy Canright, was with him at El Centro that day. Roy had a little money in Gordon's car, but the interesting thing was that he was building a Model "A" of his own and he wanted me to drive it. Roy was a slow, careful workman and an excellent, meticulous mechanic. When he had it all put together, it was a very nice car. Roy had a shop in Irvington, about half way between Oakland and San Jose. I drove his car quite a few times. Later on, Freddie Agabashian drove it, and that was his first ride in a race car with wire wheels. In earlier rides, he had spoke wheels under him.

Working with Charley Bobby was a great experience for me. I learned a lot while doing much of the work on the race car. Charley would start with a brand new Model "T" block and a supply of new connecting rods. The first thing he would do was melt out all of the bearing babbit. Then he'd drill anchor holes 1/4 inch deep in the main bearing bores and caps. These holes were located in a precise manner and tinned so as to accept the new babbit material. There was a special flux he used that worked very well with cast iron. Charley had all the fixtures and jigs needed to pour the new bearings. His choice of bearing material was something called "armature metal" and to this he added another ingredient, the nature of which I was never told. After pouring the new bearings, the block was put on the K.K. Wilson line boring equipment and the bearings cut to a slightly undersized diameter.

He had a slow turning twenty-four inch engine lathe which he fixtured to receive the Model "T" Ford block and crank. He worked out a system to provide lubrication to the bearings while they were being "burned in." Castor oil was the lubricant and Charley bought it in fifty-gallon drums. We drained it out of the race car after every race and saved it to use at the lathe. We'd secure the block and crank in the lathe, get it turning over, very slowly and then begin to tighten up the bearing caps a little at a time. Once the bearings began to smoke and squeal, the process had begun, and we let it run that way until they got quiet again and running free. Then we'd tighten it up again and there would be more smoking and more squealing. Charley said the important thing was to never stop the lathe when it was smoking and squealing, but to always wait until everything was running free. After a number of cycles of this procedure, we'd take off the caps and look at the bearing surface. It had to have a mirror finish or more of the same was called for. We were "burning in" bearings, but with a slow turning and generous use of castor oil we never did get the work hot enough to melt or damage the babbit. The one thing we did get with this system was a high conformity and precise fit between the bearing and the journal.

After we finished the main bearings, Charley had a similar procedure set up for the connecting rod bearings. We used some old dummy pistons to control the small ends of the connecting rods. We'd go through the smoking and squealing routine again until everything was smooth and bright.

The only time I know of that the Bobby Special ever lost a bearing had to do with our being rained out for a race at Fresno. The promoter there made a deal with Charley to put the car on display in the lobby of a theater for advertising purposes. The Bobby Special was a handsome little polished aluminum-bodied car, neat as a pin. The oil tank was carried under the cowl, behind the dash board. The filler neck for the tank came through the top of the cowl and was closed off with a twist cap. The gas tank was carried in the tail and was filled from there in a similar manner.

A week later, we ran the rain date. Carl Ryder was driving that Sunday. He went out, ran a few laps, and lost a bearing. When he came in, he said the oil pressure had gone down and he hadn't caught it quick enough to save it. When we got back to Watsonville and began tearing it down, we tried to drain it, but something was plugging the outlet connection. We found out that some "kook" had stuffed a scarf into the tank through the filler opening while it was on display at the theater. To my knowledge, that was the only time the Bobby ever had a bearing go bad. Charley's system for putting in bearings must have been O.K.

Charley liked to prune and pare on his connecting rods. He ground them down to where I first thought they wouldn't last one lap. When he got through, they all weighed the same and it looked like taking off one gram more would be going too far.

Of course, Charley had a pressurized oiling system in the Fronty, and he was drilling his own crankshafts. He had that operation all jigged and organized too. He broke me in on that operation and I'd do two or three crankshafts at a time. I remember the drill size being 5/32 of an inch and the special long shank drills measuring seven or eight inches. All the angles and measurements had been calculated and built into the jigs. The drill press was set on a slow speed and I used castor oil on the drill too. It was a time consuming operation, but the results were 100%—no scrap.

Charley had another little tactic he used that I'd never seen done before. He wasn't using an oil ring on the pistons, and to get away with that, everything had to fit up perfectly. Castor oil could sure foul out spark plugs in a hurry. Another trick of his was to replace only one compression ring on a piston at a time. He'd take off the top one and throw it away, move the second one up into the top groove, and put a new compression ring in the second groove. We were running four ring Ray-Day pistons at the time. When we were racing locally, the engine was taken down after every race. I wasn't sure what he was gaining with some of his tricks, but it was Charley's idea and that's the way we did it!

When we were going to run a number of races away from Watsonville and not be back between races, we would make up a number of short blocks. We would send these out ahead to those race locations. After each race, except the last, of course, we would change short blocks. The used one would be sold to any local hop-up artist who wanted it. Those fellows, whoever they might be, got some good equipment at a very fair price. The cylinder head would be transferred from block to block.

Another feature of the Bobby was a Ruckstell two speed rear axle. The lower gear was used for warming up the car and for actual racing, the taller or longer gear was called for. I could never see a great advantage to that arrangement, but it was one of Charley's pet ideas and that was that.

One of those times when Babe Stapp was back east, Mel Kenealy was driving the car. It was during a preliminary heat race that Mel came down the home straight full bore and about threw the car into the first turn backwards. Charley looked at me and said, "Did you see that? What the devil's going on?" I saw it alright and was puzzled too. Just before the feature race was to begin, Charley had me go down into the corner to see what was taking place. Charley's suspicions proved to be correct. The shifting lever for the Ruckstell was about a foot long and on the left side of the car. The hand brake for the two rear wheels was longer and on the right-hand side. Mel came flying into the corner, reached down with his left hand, and snapped the Ruckstell into low gear. He really had it crossed up going through the turn. I reported back to Charley what I'd seen. He told me not to let on to Mel that we knew what he was doing. "We'll fix that so-and-so," he said. After the race, Mel went back to Los Angeles and we returned to Watsonville. The very next day, we took the rear axle down and ground off the internal shift lock on the low side. After that, if you wanted it to be in low range you'd have to hold it there. That sort of spoiled it for Mel. When he came off the track at the next event, he asked Charley, with a chuckle in his voice, "What'd you do to it, Charley?" Charley answered, "All I did was put a stop to you racing my car in low gear." There wasn't anymore said about it after that.

The magneto on the Bobby came off of a twin ignition Stutz.

The Bobby The Babe and Me

There was a fellow in Watsonville who ran an auto electric shop and who was a dealer for the Bosch line. This guy was interested in racing, and Charley's work was always welcome into his shop. I don't doubt he made the extra effort to do the best job possible for Charley. He re-wound the Stutz magneto to be compatible with the higher r.p.m.s it would be turning. There was also some work he did on the input drive that made it better for Charley's use as well as more reliable. When he finished, it threw fire like I had never seen before. That rebuilt magneto contributed a lot to our spark plugs' ability to resist fouling.

In the old days, Champion plugs were all that Charley used. He made a little device, using two sockets to take them apart. Once an upper threaded ring was removed, the porcelain element came right out. A pair of copper gaskets, one on each side of a shoulder on the porcelain, sealed off the combustion chamber pressures. Another one of my jobs was to take those plugs apart and clean them. I'd polish them with alcohol and a rag until the porcelain just shone. There was no such thing as sandblasting plugs back then. We set the plug gap at .035, which we considered to be quite wide, but we had the magneto to get the job done.

We didn't know anything at all about "heat ranges" on spark plugs. When Babe Stapp returned from Indianapolis one year, he brought back the story on that. He came in with a well-made, finely-finished wood cabinet about the size of a machinists tool box. I think his father put it together. It was nicely compartmented on the inside and was filled with sets of spark plugs of all different specifications—a real good assortment. Babe went into an explanation about "heat ranges" and how you go about selecting the proper one. He explained to us how you could vary the heat range by varying the thickness of the gasket on the end of the plug or by using several gaskets. This was all new and interesting information for us at the time.

We were all trying to run higher compression ratios in our engines then, and doping our fuel with benzol was one of the ways of doing that. One time Babe came in with a little bottle of liquid that was very heavy for its size, and we were curious as the devil about that. Babe told us all about it, but we were to keep the information to ourselves. He'd acquired this fluid from an old-time race driver named Frank Elliot, who'd gone to work for the Ethyl Corporation. It was a big hush-hush deal, so we were to keep it under our hat. This stuff was supposed to be a much better additive for our fuel than benzol. Babe told us about how much was to be used with five gallons of gasoline. Babe and Charley mixed up some test batches of fuel and then checked the results by reading the color of the spark plugs. When they arrived at a certain color, they felt they had just the right proportions. Charley was very fussy about mixing his race fuel, just like he was about most things and it seemed to pay off for him. We used it in the race car and it worked better than benzol. If we could get a steady supply of this Ethyl fluid, there wouldn't be a need for any more benzol. Looking back now, I can see how innocent we were about getting those fuel-doping chemicals on us when we mixed up our racing gas. We didn't think a thing about it. These days, gloves, masks and who knows what else would be the order of the day to even get close to some of that stuff.

We used up the first little bottle of Ethyl after awhile. In the meantime, one of our friends who knew a mechanic who worked for an air carrier over in Monterey came up with a quart of the additive. We were then well supplied, and getting the jump on some of our competition. All of this took place before Ethyl was an advertised product and generally available.

A fellow named Fisher came over from Denver to race with us at San Jose. He had an SR Fronty and I believe Johnny Kreiger was driving it. The first time out on the track, the Saturday before the race, he blew a piston. So they tipped the car up on two of its wheels and went to work putting in a new piston. They went out again, ran a few laps and holed another piston. Fisher could see that we had practically the same set-up on our car as he did on his, so he came over to talk to Charley. He wanted to know what we thought his problem might be. Charley was always willing to help in situations like this, so he asked Fisher what compression ratio he was running and Fisher told him, "About ten to one."

Charley said, "Ten to one? Good Lord man, I'm running eight to one and figure I'm on the very edge." Charley looked at him thoughtfully for a moment and asked, "You're from Denver aren't you?"

"Right, I am," Fisher answered.

"Well, Denver's up there pretty high isn't it?" Charley went on.

"Sure," said Fisher, "A mile high."

Charley replied, "Good God, man, you're down to sea level here and that ten to one is way out of line."

They talked things over and found out that the two cars were running the same cylinder bore size. Charley said to me, "Herk, you hurry on back to Watsonville and get that spare set of pistons off the shelf. Bring a set of rings for them, too." Fisher got into my little hopped-up Chevy with me and we went tearing down the highway together. After we got back, Fisher put in that set of lower compression pistons and had no more trouble. He ran the whole race and was amused afterwards about how he hadn't taken compression increase and altitude difference into account. Charley had picked up on it right away.

In those days, the guys always helped each other out when they could. I remember the time Art Sparks was trying to run an old Winfield flat head Ford at Fresno and he came over to Charley for help. He wanted Charley to time the engine for him. Charley looked at him with some disbelief and said, "Sure, but I'll bet you can do it." At that time, Sparks must have felt that Charley knew much more about it than he did, or maybe he was trying to get some information out of Charley on the sly. Sparks later moved up to an SR Fronty and then much bigger, better and faster cars after that. Everything has a beginning. I thought about that incident many times as Sparks came to be a power in racing at the highest level.

Another job I had while working on Charley's race car was

balancing the Buffalo wire wheels. We took a spare front spindle and hub, put in new lightly oiled bearings and fastened it to a bracket on the edge of the work bench so the wheel was free to rotate. If the wheel stopped in the same place a number of times, I'd mark the heavy spot with chalk and then go to the spoke exactly opposite and wrap on some wire solder. I'd go ahead that way until I got the wheel so that it would never stop in the same place. I spent a lot of time balancing wheels for Charley, and Charley had a lot of wheels.

The Buffalo wire wheels had a tendency, on occasion, to have their lock rings pop off and that could wreck a race car in a hurry. As a safety measure, I'd drill five equally spaced 1/8 inch holes around the circumference of the ring and wheel and put in cotter pins. This was Charley's idea, too, and I guess it must have worked because we never lost a lock ring.

Charley also installed over-sized cylinder head studs in the Ford block. The Fronty head he was running had two Siamesed intake ports with a stud running through each of them. He had ground out those ports until it would scare you. He flattened out the studs where they passed through the port until they were strut shaped, streamlined and offered less resistance to the charge coming in. I don't believe they were as much as a quarter-inch thick at their thickest. We never broke either of those studs, so that worked out O.K. too.

The Bobby ran a single two-inch Zenith carburetor which seemed monstrous to me at the time. I couldn't get over the size of that hole. Babe Stapp was a great friend of Eddie Winfield. After he'd been driving for Charley for awhile, he came up from Los Angeles with a pair of Winfield down drafts. These were the older Model "S" that an outfit called Hammel-Gherke in Los Angeles had converted. They had turned the bowls over and made some other modifications. Babe was sure they'd be better than the single Zenith, but he had quite a job convincing Charley to try them. Charley finally agreed, with some reluctance, to go along with Babe and that meant making up a new intake manifold and throttle linkage. Babe won the very next race with the Winfields on, but Charley still wasn't convinced. The following race was with the Zenith and Babe won again. That was quite a game Babe and Charley played switching carburetors back and forth. The last time I saw the car, it had on the Zenith. Babe was driving other cars, so it looked like Charley won that game, but not as many races any more.

Charley was always concerned with rear axle gear ratios. He had nine, ten and eleven tooth pinion gears and three different sizes of wheels and tires for the rear. When we got to a track where we hadn't been before, he wouldn't say a whole lot. He'd light up a cigarette, take a walk around the track, look everything over, and then come back and tell us what he thought we should put on the car. He'd send the driver out for a few laps and then bring him in and ask a lot of questions. He wanted to know how it felt to the driver, how many r.p.m.s he was getting at a certain place on the track, and things of that sort. In some cases, we'd have to tip the car up on its side and change the final drive ratio. Everybody else was doing more or less the same thing. Every time we changed something, the driver would have to take it out, try it, and give Charley a detailed report. Between the three pinion gears and the three wheel and tire sizes, we had nine combinations to try—whatever he decided. I always felt Charley made the right choice with fewer changes than most owners. It made a lot of work for the pit crew, but that is where much of the serious racing is done and it paid off. When we got to a track where we'd raced before or raced a lot, like San Jose, Charley already knew how he wanted the car set-up and the car was basically ready when we got to the track. With these modern quick-change rear ends, we really would have had a ball.

Back in 1929, when we were still flat-towing the Bobby with the big, old Nash Ambassador, Charley decided we should go over to Phoenix, Arizona, during the State Fair for a race. We got everything all loaded up and I mean it was L-O-A-D-E-D! There was Charley, Babe, myself and a fellow named Bill Hughes, who hung around the shop. We stopped at Pismo Beach on the way down and had a libation with one of Charley's bootlegger friends. When we got to Babe's place in Los Angeles, we met Babe's brother-in-law who worked for Bekins Transfer Company. He looked us over and thought he could make a lot of room available inside the Nash by tying the extra race car wheels and some other things onto the side of the race car. We had already taken the trunk off the luggage rack at the back of the Nash and replaced it with a bigger box that we'd built. We were still crowded. The brother-in-law, a moving expert, began lashing things to the side of the race car. Charley watched all this with doubt on his face, and voiced the opinion that some of the stuff was sure to fall off before we got to Phoenix. The answer by the mover was, "If any of it comes off, I'll come down personally, put it on my back, and carry it wherever you want it to go." Well, he lashed the things on so good that when we got to Phoenix, nothing had even moved. Trouble was that we didn't have him there to load up for the return trip. We couldn't come close to doing the job that he had done and we had a mess. We fought that stuff all the way back.

The race at Phoenix would be under the control of that AAA stalwart, Fred "Pop" Wagner, and well contested with a field of twenty five entries. Among the "Hot Shoes" who'd had or would later have Indianapolis 500 driving experience were Babe Stapp, Francis Quinn, Johnny Kreiger, Al Gordon, "Stubby" Stubblefield, Mel Kenealy, and Lou Moore. Lou Moore would also be a winning car owner. Fred Frame, who went on to win the 1932 Indy 500, was also there. Other strong and experienced drivers were Arvol Brunmier, "Speed" Hinckley, Walt May and Jimmy Sharp.

Babe Stapp, in the #25 Bobby Special, set the pace early in the day with a qualifying lap of 43 seconds flat (83.79 mph), lowering the prior record of Ralph DePalma by a full second. Stubblefield in the #18 Simplex Special was next fastest in qualifying with a time of 44.2 seconds. "Speed" Hinckley took the #11 Evans Paramount Special through the fence on the south turn during his time trial and wound up with shoulder injuries. He didn't get tossed out of the cockpit, but the car was a mess and done for the day.

The program consisted of four 5-mile heats and a 40-mile feature race. The fastest one-half of the qualifiers went into the first heat, and Babe won that at a speed of 84 m.p.h. Stubblefield was second in the Simplex and Jimmy Sharp in the Mahoney Special was third.

The second heat consisted of the non-winners of the first heat, plus the next three fastest qualifiers. The winner was Fred Frame in the #33 Barney Special at a speed of 80.86 m.p.h. He was followed across the line, 3/10ths of a second later by Francis Quinn in the #58 Miller. Third was Johnny Kreiger in the Fisher Special #82.

The third 5-mile heat was composed of the non-winners of the first two heats plus the next three fastest qualifiers. This heat was won by Al Gordon in the #46 Morris Special at a speed of 78.84 m.p.h. He was followed by Ray Gardner in his #73 Gardner Special and Walt May in the #47 Multi-Ford Special.

The fourth and final heat was for those who didn't make it into the first three heats. It was won by Tony Radetich in the #13 Jerome Special at 77.12 m.p.h. Phil Pardee in the #41 Edington Special and Mel Kenealy in the #6 Redlands Special followed.

Fifteen cars started the 40-mile main event and Babe Stapp was impressive in the Bobby. He led every lap, made no pit stops, and won handily averaging 80.55 m.p.h.

Francis Quinn in the Miller hit the fence in the north turn on lap eleven, but pulled his car back onto the track and continued. Lap thirty five was another bad one for Quinn. He lost it coming onto the main straight, got out of shape and went thru the inside fence. He wasn't hurt, but the #58 Miller was ready for the infirmary.

Stubblefield pressed Babe hard early in the race and then faded. The next challenger was Devon Smith in the Begg

Special. Babe sort of let him run hub to hub until one of Smith's tires went down and he had to spend forty seconds in the pits being re-shod. Fred Frame then came up from third place in the Barney machine, and Babe showed him the way around the race track. There was never any doubt in our minds about who was the boss out there that day. Our car was running so good at the end of the race that it seemed like we could have kept right on running until dark. Besides a qualifying record, Babe also set a new 40-mile time for the Phoenix mile track.

Fred Frame broke a connecting rod on the last lap and still managed to finish second. He caught fire coming in after the checkered flag and had to be extinguished when he got back to his pit. I'd say that was a pretty toasty cool-off lap.

Smith gave it all he had and was able to make up much of the pit stop deficit. He came home third behind Frame in a surviving field of eight cars.

On that November day in 1929 at Phoenix, Babe Stapp took everything except Pop Wagner's watch. I know that Babe, Charley, Bill Hughes and I were on cloud nine and not caring if there was a cloud ten!

These were prohibition times, and on the return trip, we had to go through a checking station near the California line at Yuma, Arizona. We got to that place about two o'clock in the morning, the wind was howling and it was cold. The temperature wasn't actually so low, but with all that wind it got you to shivering.

For some reason known only to him, Babe started giving the inspector a lot of guff and he did it well. We wound up having to unload every darn thing we had. He gave us the "fine toothed comb" treatment. He went through all of our suitcases, tool boxes, and every nook and cranny in the Nash and the race car—the works! Then we had to reload it, all out in the cold. Charley was so mad at Babe for that stunt that if it hadn't been for our clean sweep at Phoenix, he could have killed him or at least tried. Quoting Charley, "If he'd a kept his damned mouth shut we'd got through there in nothing flat." Maybe Babe was still feeling a little frisky after his big win. If he had a point to make, I don't know what it was, but the inspector made sure we understood who was in charge.

We came to a fork in the road and Babe said, "Let's go over into Mexico and look around." Charley was concerned about all the money we were carrying. Phoenix had paid in cash. Charley and Babe had the big bills in their shoes. Charley finally agreed, and we went into a place called Algadones. We hit a few joints, looked around a little and then headed into Los Angeles. We dropped Babe off at his place and the three of us drove back to Watsonville, another 350 miles or so.

In 1930, it was decided that we would make a circuit and run a series of four races that included Phoenix before returning home. There would be additional races for us at San Jose, Oakland, and other places where we'd be back to Watsonville the same day. First on our schedule was Bakersfield, then Ascot at Los Angeles, followed by Imperial, and then on to Phoenix. Charley couldn't make the whole swing, so Babe and I left without him. He was to catch up with us later. We were flat towing the race car again as we had in 1929. Charley had sent out the short blocks so we'd be able to change engines quickly after each race. We had that down to a "fire drill"! When we were in Los Angeles, we always stayed at Babe's place. After the Imperial race, we parked the race car in a local garage. One of the guys hanging around there advised us that if we were going to head over to Phoenix, we'd better be doing it then because he figured there was a dust storm coming up. Babe told him that we were going to change the engine the next day and then run over to Phoenix.

We got back to the garage the following morning and were changing the engine when this same guy came in and said, "If I were you guys, I wouldn't be starting out today. It sure don't look good." Well, we did start out, and after awhile we could see a big yellow dust cloud up ahead. Babe said, "Uh-oh!, we'd better stop and cover the race car engine." Babe had a very fine imported camel hair coat he took out and wrapped over the engine, covering the carburetors and other vital spots. We started out again, and we didn't get very far when it got so bad we couldn't see a thing. So, we pulled over to the side of the road and sat there for several hours with the windows rolled up. When the storm finally blew itself out, the windshield was so sandblasted we couldn't see a thing out of it. The driver's side window was the same way. We drove the rest of the way by taking turns behind the wheel and looking forward out of the side window. It wasn't too comfortable, but nothing else could be done. When we got to Phoenix, we had the windshield and driver's side door glass replaced.

We were worried, too, about how the race car engine had made it through the dust storm. Babe was optimistic about it, having taken the precaution of covering it up with his fine imported camel hair coat. When we got the engine uncovered, I could see dust in the carburetors. So we took off the intake manifold, with carburetors, and I could see dust in the intake ports. We heated up the crankcase with a blow torch and drained the castor oil out of it. We got hold of a couple gallons of alcohol, sloshed it around and got everything cleaned up the best we could. We were concerned about not getting all of the dust out, but on the other hand, it was very fine dust and maybe a little of it in there wouldn't hurt anything either. We were racing the car on dirt, and some big industrial engines had their rings broken in by letting them inhale a little Bon Ami. Anyway, just for the heck of it, I saved a jug of that dirty alcohol and when the dust had settled out we had about a half inch of sediment on the bottom.

Babe won everything at Phoenix again, his heat and the feature too, the same way he did in 1929. He took the whole show and I think there were forty cars there, including guys from back east. It was quite a gathering.

The Phoenix VFW, a very active local group, put on the program and they did a great job. They also threw a big banquet the evening after the race which was worth remembering. I recall sitting with Harvey Ward, Shorty Cantlon, and Roscoe Ford. Charley Bobby made it to Phoenix for the race, attended the dinner, and returned home with us. Babe dropped off at his home in Los Angeles and Charley and I drove back to Watsonville without incident, quietly enjoying the good fortune we'd had at Phoenix.

When I first went to work for Charley, we were flat-towing the race car to the track with a big Nash. He had his Nash agency in the front of the building and the shop was in the rear. We towed down for a race at Imperial one time, and there we saw a rig some guy had brought out from back East, a truck set up to be a race car transporter. When Charley saw that, he said, "Boy, that's the way to go!" When we got back to Watsonville, things started to happen. Charley had a big old Hudson Super Six sitting around which was just what we needed. He took off the back half of the body and extended the frame rails. There was an old fellow who used to hang around the shop named Bill Williams. He was interested in the race car and went with us to most all of the races. He was quite handy, and when Charley was ready for him, he went to work on the project. He made a flat bed, built up the sides with storage compartments for tools and things, and built a rack for wheels and tires and ramps to drive the race car up on. There were two sets of turnbuckles to hold the car in place. Bill Williams sure did a fine job setting up that transporter. Charley had to have everything first class, so he finished off the job with a beautiful blue and white paint job. After the transporter was finished, we practiced loading and unloading the race car until we had it down pat.

Our first trip with the new rig was down to a race at Los Angeles. Babe and I were to go down ahead, and Charley was to follow a day or so later. We got as far as Salinas and blew one of a set of brand new tires that were put on before we left Watsonville. Babe said, "We'd better call Charley and tell him about this. We really shouldn't go any farther without a spare." We found a telephone and got hold of Charley. He said, "O.K., I'll bring down a couple of more spares. You guys just keep going and I'll catch up with you." So, we got down around Gonzales or Solidad and blew another tire. Babe said, "Herk, there's something wrong going on here. We're only going 45 or 50 miles an hour and that can't be the problem." Babe called Charley again and caught him just as he was about to leave. Charley said for us to sit tight. He was going to call the tire man in Watsonville and see what he could find out. Charley called back after awhile and said the tire man told him we were putting too much weight on the size of tire we were using. The only thing for us to do was to pick up some tires locally and hold our speed down to about 30 miles -an-hour. We nursed it along and got to Los Angeles without any more tire trouble. When we arrived, Babe got in touch with a friend of his who put on bigger and better rubber, so we wouldn't have to creep along like we were going to a funeral. That trip was a memorable initiation for the new transporter.

In 1931, a bunch of cars and drivers from the east came to run the inaugural race on the Oakland mile. Louis Schneider had won the Indy 500, and he was one of that group. He was driving a Stagger Valve Fronty that the Chevrolet brothers built and owned. This had an unusual cylinder head design. It was sixteen valves with an intake and exhaust valve on each side of the combustion chamber. The intakes were located diagonally opposite each other as were the exhaust valves. This arrangement was to provide a swirling turbulence within the cylinder. It required intake and exhaust manifolds on both sides of the head. It was thought that this design would result in a big step ahead in engine output. I don't know that it ever lived up to that promise.

The out-of-town guys were all staying at the same hotel, and that's where the driver's meeting was held the night before the race. After the meeting, we were all standing around in little groups talking about this and that. Babe was nearby talking to someone I didn't recognize. He motioned me over and introduced me to Art Chevrolet. Art told me he was going to have a little party up in his room and wanted to get hold of some whiskey, a gallon if possible. I told him I was quite well acquainted around Oakland and thought I could get what he wanted. He gave me some money and away I went.

I got the gallon of booze in short order and took it up to Art Chevrolet's room. Louis Schneider, who apparently had his own supply of liquor was up there too, had been drinking a little too much and was kind of making an "ass" of himself. He was with a fellow called Alabam, who was over in the corner playing a harmonica for the group and doing a good job of it. I got to talking to Chevrolet, and he said, "Oh! You're the fellow that's been with Babe Stapp on the Bobby car. What's it got in it?" I told him it was just a single stick eight valve Fronty. His reply: "I don't understand how an eight valve can run that fast. What kind of a crank does it have?" He couldn't figure out how we were able to do what we did with what we had. Nothing I was able to tell him cleared it up. "You know," he said, "When Babe was back at Indianapolis, he told us about how well it went and I swore I had to see that car." I told him that Babe and the Bobby would be there tomorrow, and he could see it at the track. I don't know if he ever got a good look at car or had a chance to talk to Charley Bobby. I also don't know if he thought I was giving him straight answers. The funny part of it is, I was.

Besides working with the Bobby, I was driving Roy Canright's Miller-Schofield the following day and was able to finish ahead of Louis Schneider in the Stagger Valve Fronty. Some other drivers and I probably felt better about that than we had a right to. Schneider's car wasn't running right and that was no fault of his. It was just something to talk about.

Babe Stapp came back from Indianapolis in 1931 with stories about a Tucker Tappet car that was based on a Model "A" block and was supposed to be pretty good. In the latter part of that year, we went to Bakersfield for a two-day, Saturday and Sunday, race meet. Charley didn't go down with us—other pressing matters. Paul Durkham, a business man around Bakersfield and quite active in community affairs, was promoting the races. Paul was putting on a Friday night dinner and entertainment at the Elk's Club. He had invited a number of race car guys, including Louie Meyer. The dinner was about over and Louie hadn't arrived yet. The topic of conversation was Babe and Cotton Henning's recent trip to Europe.

All of a sudden, in burst Louie Meyer and Riley Brett all out of breath. Babe asked, "What's the matter? You guys get hung-up somewhere?" Riley answered, "Look, I'll tell you fellows, but don't you ever let it out. Louie and I were doing some last minute things on the race car (a new eight-cylinder 220) and Louie's wife wanted to take the tow car to do some shopping. He told her to go ahead, but be sure to fill it up with gas on her way back. When she got back we hooked up the race car and took off. We got almost to the top on the Ridge Route and it quit on us. We fiddled and fooled around and fiddled some more. We went so far as disconnecting the fuel pump before we discovered we were out of gas. Somebody came along who had a little spare gas and helped us get going. Don't you guys ever tell anybody about this. Louie's wife forgot to put in the gas and maybe the gas guage wasn't working either."

Anyhow, after some fifty-odd years, I think Louie would forgive me for telling about it now.

When we got to the track at Bakersfield, Louie and Riley already had the new eight-cylinder 220 running. They had built this car for Indy and just brought it to Bakersfield to try it out. Shorty Cantlon was driving it that day. He was out there buzzing around with a bunch of other cars, in practice, when suddenly, everyone looked over to the turn to see Shorty doing a couple of gilhooleys. We didn't find out until a day later what had caused the problem. They'd forgot to pin a big crankcase nut on the front of the crankshaft. It had worked loose and allowed the crankshaft to slide back and ruin the main bearing webs. That was all for their car on that trip.

Billy Arnold was out on the track in the Tucker Tappet car,

and Babe was watching it with interest. I was checking this, that and the other on the Bobby and was also aware of how well Billy Arnold was getting around. He was really moving, and Babe and I both knew it. After Babe went out for warm-up and practice, he came back in and said, "Herk, I think we've just had the panties hung on us." Babe called Charley in Watsonville and told him all about it. Charley hit the roof, jumped into his Nash, and he was down to Bakersfield, pronto. When he got to the track, he lit into both of us; we hadn't done this and we hadn't done that and so on. Well, Charley checked everything and did everything he could think of to do. We still weren't fast enough to stay with the Tucker Tappet. Arnold had several miles an hour on us. We beat everybody but him. We couldn't touch him. This was the first time I'd seen the Bobby beat like that and it was like somebody in the family died!

On the way home, Charley told Babe that he was going to build a Model "A" Ford engine for the Bobby. In response, Babe said he'd talk to Eddie Winfield for some inside dope. I had just witnessed the beginning of the end for the Bobby and didn't realize it at the time. Charley's heart was broken. He continued to talk about building a new engine, but nothing ever happened. Every time I'd bring up the subject, he'd say, "Herk, we'll just have to wait a while with that," and nothing continued to happen.

After Bakersfield, Babe could see that Charley's heart just wasn't in it any more. So he and Charley went their separate ways. We had a race coming at Oakland, and Francis Quinn came up from Los Angeles to drive the Bobby. He went out on the track to warm it up and try it out, and it began sputtering. This was something very unusual for the Bobby to do, because it always ran very solid. The only time it hadn't was at Fresno when we found the scarf in the oil tank. Quinn came in and Charley checked it over very briefly and said, "That's it, that's all for the day. Load her up!" Francis Quinn was killed on highway 99 near Fresno as he was returning to Los Angeles, so he never really got to drive the car. The date was December 13, 1931.

Babe and the Bobby

When we got back to the shop and took the engine down, we found we'd sheared a pin in the cam drive causing the valve timing to go sour. I took the car apart, but never got to put it back together again. Charley may have figured the gods had forsaken him with the car. His new interest was in firearms and seeing the handwriting on the wall, I took another job. I couldn't stand being that close to a race car that wasn't doing what it was meant to do. I missed the action.

I was in the 1932 New Year's Day race on the Oakland Mile, when Fred "Pop" Wagner got hurt. I remember Babe Stapp, Bryan Saulpaugh and Ralph Hepburn running in the event and there were others too. Ralph Hepburn broke an axle during the race, got into the outside wall and came back down scattering race car pieces all over the track. Wagner got out the yellow flag and we ran that way for about twenty-seven laps. Oakland was an oiled track, something like macadam or black-top. It would get very slippery when wet. While under the yellow, a kind of a very warm moist air mass drifted in from Oakland Bay and some of it condensed on the track surface. Stapp and Saulpaugh were up ahead. I was hanging back, waiting and watching, probably a lap down. When Pop Wagner dropped the green flag, I had the best seat in the house to see what was about to take place. Those two up ahead just stood on it right now, broke loose and got sideways. Babe got way down, almost into the pits, then back across the track nearly into the wall before he was able to get it settled down. With Saulpaugh, it all happened much quicker. When it got sideways on him, he became a passenger in his own race car, slid to the inside and took out the elevated starter's platform that was cantilevered out over the track. Pop Wagner came crashing to the ground with it. The telephone that was up there on a little table came down too and struck Wagner on the head. I was back far enough to be able to see it all and still have time to slow up a bit and not get involved. I went around once and pulled into the pit and the race was black-flagged.

I heard it said that the injuries Wagner suffered that day were responsible for his death somewhat later. It was not a very good day for any of us.

Saulpaugh's injuries were serious enough to put him in the hospital for awhile. On the positive side was the mutual attraction that developed between him and a nurse that was on duty there. Once he got to moving around again, they were seen in each other's company. I don't know how that relationship evolved, if at all. Brian Saulpaugh was killed at Oakland, California on April 22, 1933.

In 1928 Jack Buxton won the Pacific Coast Dirt Track Championship driving the Bobby Special. He also drove relief for Herman Schurch at Indy in 1929.

(Krause Collection)

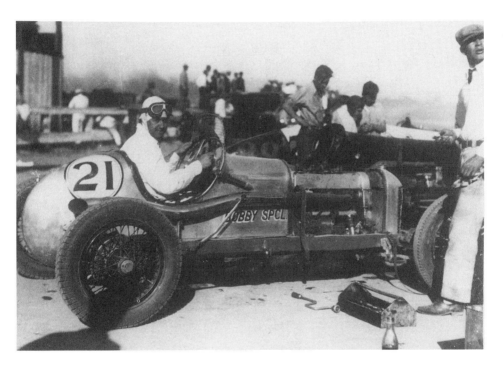

Babe Stapp, "The Bobby," and Herk Edwards. This is the only known photo of the three together.

Babe Stapp and the Duesenberg at Indianapolis in 1931.

Babe Stapp and Charlie Bobby at Ascot on Nov. 24, 1929.

Indianapolis veteran, Mel Kenealy, in the Bobby at San Jose in 1932.

#48 Arvol Brunmeir in Harvey Ward's Marine Miller on the pole.
#9 Mel Kenealy in "The Bobby" outside on the front row.

(Burgess Collection)

Speed Hinckley in "The Bobby."

Babe Stapp in "The Bobby."

Babe Stapp

INDIANAPOLIS 500 RECORD

YEAR	Finish	Laps	Car
1927	31	24	Duesenberg
1928	6	200	Miller
1929	28	40	Spindler-Miller
1930	31	18	Duesenberg
1931	35	9	Rigling-Henning
1933	23	156	Boyle Products
1935	25	70	Marks-Miller
1936	24	89	Pirrung
1937	31	36	Topping
1938	26	54	McCoy Auto Service
1939	5	200	Alfa Romeo
1940	24	64	Surber

Little, Big and Bigger

After leaving Charley Bobby, I took a job with Harold Kundson at his Chevrolet garage in Watsonville. I wasn't there very long when a fellow named Cunningham came over from Salt Lake City and bought the Kundson business. It then became the Cunningham Chevrolet Agency and at that time I took over as service foreman.

A fellow from Fresno who was working for me had a friend that was coming up from there with one of those new midget race cars. I was told they were getting to be quite popular. Heck, I'd never seen one and didn't even know what they were. The fellow with the midget showed up and what he had was a three-cylinder Chevy—a six-cylinder he'd cut in half. It was called the "Shutz Body Works Special" and Vern Gardner was driving it for him. He wanted to show it to us, and I wanted to hear it run, so they unloaded it and drove it around on the next door service station lot. They were headed for Alviso, just above San Jose, to race that night, so some of us decided to go over there and see them run.

It wasn't much of a track, but in those days just about anything would do, and this was one of the first in our part of the country. I think it was set up on an old ball diamond and for a night race, they came up a little short on lighting. I watched those races and it sure looked like a lot of fun. I'd say I got hooked!

A couple of nights later, they were going to race at the San Francisco Motor Drome, a converted dog track, so we went over there too. Vern Gardner, the driver of that three-cylinder Chevy, came over and invited me to take the car out on the track and try it. "You'll get a kick out of it," he said. I was more than willing, and the last thing he told me was to watch out for the quick steering. "It's not like a big car," he warned. Well, I'd been driving dirt track cars for awhile and I thought to myself, there can't be anything to driving these playthings. I'll show these kids how to do it! I went out there and the very first time, I got on it and came into the corner hot.

It spun three times!

I came in sort of humbled, everyone was laughing and Vern said, "No, Herk, that isn't the way to do it!" That was my "not so great" introduction to midget race cars.

While I was there at the San Francisco Motor Drome, a fellow named Charles DeCosta came over and introduced himself. He wanted to know if I was the same Edwards that was driving the big cars. He said that he had an auto repair shop over in Oakland and was building a four-port Riley—it was about ready to go and was I interested? I indicated some interest. The car actually belonged to a boxer named Joe Armstrong who'd been paying all the bills. His ring career was going well, so there was no cash flow problem. There was also some help from Scott Neilson, who had a Nash-Cord dealership in Berkeley. His company's name and location were lettered on the side of the cowl.

I agreed to take it over to the Oakland Speedway on a Sunday and try it out. Like most new cars just out of the box it had some bugs, but I could also see that it had possibilities.

This was sort of an unsettled time for me. Things weren't working out too well at the Cunningham Garage in Watsonville. DeCosta had also asked about my mechanical experience and ability, indicating that if I wanted to come up to Oakland and work for him, there would be a place for me. That was all it took. I went back to Watsonville, gathered up my tools and personal things and went to work for DeCosta in Oakland.

Little, Big and Bigger

Midget racing was gaining ground, and Emoryville's converted dog track became a popular place. I also got tied in with a guy who was finishing up a midget car. Even though I had big car experience, to be able to run in midgets, it was required that I run in some training races. Maybe I had proven the need for that on my earlier night at the Motor Drome. Once I got the O.K. to drive midgets, my schedule got a little crowded. I was running big cars on Sunday, midgets during the week, doing customer work in the garage and maintaining the Riley dirt car in my spare time. I wasn't making much money racing, but I guess I thought I was having lots of fun. Maybe it got to be too much.

The Riley deal was starting to come unglued. Not all of the money that Armstrong advanced to buy things for the car was being spent that way. DeCosta's credibility began to suffer with me and maybe with Armstrong too. The car went good while it lasted. I'd win a heat race or a trophy race, and then some damn thing would fall off the car in the main event and I'd be out of it. Anything DeCosta did on the car had to be gone over. I couldn't trust him. As it turned out, he was being paid for work that I was doing on my free time. I was getting no place in a hurry with the Armstrong car, so I began to drive for other big car owners when I had the chance. Eventually the situation soured completely, and I left DeCosta to work for Scott Neilson in the shop of his Nash-Cord dealership in Berkeley. DeCosta gave up on the car, and it was sold to another fellow in Oakland. I lost track of it.

Scott Neilson was keen on racing, and that must have been one of the reasons I went to work for him. Racing midgets three or four nights a week and big cars on weekends had me going like a brace and bit. Then the next thing to make the racing scene were stock cars under the promotion of Charley Currier. I got involved in that when Scott Neilson asked me which one of the cars his dealership was selling did I think would be best for racing? I told him that the best way to determine that was to take one of each out to the Oakland Speedway and give them a try. I got hold of Charlie Currier and made arrangements to use the track. He was an accommodating fellow and a real nice guy.

We took out a lightweight six-cylinder Nash LaFayette, a big used Nash six-cylinder with a Monitor engine, and a front drive Cord that Scott was driving as a demonstrator. We met Currier at the track and after bringing up the tire pressures, went out with the big Nash. It wasn't too fast, but steady. I found I could put my foot in it all the way around without lifting, and it handled very well.

The little LaFayette was lively. Its engine wound up tighter, about a half-second faster, but not nearly as sure-footed on the track. It bounced a lot and wasn't as steady.

Neilson wanted me to take the Cord around too. It was geared too tall, and when I flicked the electric shift into third gear, it wound up too tight and didn't go anyplace. It just wasn't geared right, and it didn't seem like there was going to be much we were going to be able to do about that.

When Scott asked me what I thought, I told him the big Nash would most likely be the best bet. He agreed, so we decided to go to work on it. Scott was going to try for some factory support, but he also realized he might have to do it on his own. He was willing to try.

I was working in the shop and also in charge of the cars on the used car lot. There was some flexibility in the use of my time and a race for stock cars was coming up soon, so I went to work on the big Nash.

We took the fenders off, replaced the shock absorbers and generally got it ready in what little time was left. Next to the Nash agency was the Dempsey and Sanders Goodyear Tire store. Goodyear was having a big promotion on their "Lifeguard" inner tubes, so we worked out a deal where they furnished the tires and tubes and put them on for us. During the race, the track became quite rough, and when I got into traffic and was forced to run out of the groove, I hit a big hole. That bent the tie rod and put the front wheels way out of line. With all of that "tow-out," the car was unmanageable, and it was just all over the place. I tried it for a couple of laps, but it was just hog wild. When I came into the pits one of the guys got down on the ground, looked under the front end and yelled, "Oh, crap, you really bent hell out of that tie rod!" Well, I suspected that. They got under there with an iron bar, hammered on it, pried on it and got it somewhat straightened out. All we could do was to try it again. So I went back out. It was better, but it sure didn't feel like it should. The wheels were so far out of line that the tread was scuffing off the outside edges. I was on the back straight when I heard and felt a front tire let go. I brought the car around and into the pits with the tire down, but not totally flat. Well, that was exactly what Dempsey and Sanders and their cameraman needed, but we sure didn't. The guys put on new front tires and away we went. With all of that monkey business, we still managed to get a third out of that race.

The fast V-8 Fords were always running hot and over-cooking. Some finished the race running on half their cylinders, and some didn't finish at all.

According to the rules, you could change or improve anything that had to do with safety. One of the first things we did was to stiffen up that Nash tie rod.

After the race, the Goodyear people took some more photographs to plug their "Lifeguard" inner tube. My picture, with the story, appeared in the Goodyear Newsletter that was circulated to all the dealers. A Letter of Authorization was given to me for a ride in the Goodyear Blimp, but I never got around to doing that. I was told that the "Lifeguard" equipped tire on the Nash was the first to have a blowout under actual use conditions. Others, under test conditions, had been blown out with shotgun blasts or other explosive charges. My experience with the tube took place before a large crowd of people, so that made it all the better. Who could argue with that?

The next idea they came up with was to have someone run over a pair of spiked planks with all four wheels. They wanted to know if I'd be interested in doing that. I told them, sure, I'd try it. Charley Currier said we'd have to do this on the Q.T., because his insurance wouldn't cover anything like that. Before we did anything, he had us all sign waivers. They laid the planks out on the home straight, and I ran across then a couple of times at a pretty good speed. The tires stayed up just as they were supposed to. Well, the next thought was to have me do this at a race meet in front of the crowd and get all that publicity. In thinking more about it, we had to take old William Randolph Hearst into account. Another driver had recently been killed, and Hearst had been coming down on auto racing pretty hard in his newspaper. After some sober reflection, Charley Currier said we'd better not take a chance—run the risk of someone getting hurt and having it wind up in the newspapers. We didn't need that kind of publicity.

That big Nash was like a Mack truck. I could stand on it all the way around and something had to be done about that. We needed more acceleration and straightaway speed. There were a lot of guys who knew the Fords inside out. If you had a fast one and they looked you over or tore you down, they'd find out in a hurry if you were "legal." We figured we might get away with a little on the Nash—no one else was running one.

The Nash had what was called the "Monitor" motor, a big rugged six that never gave up. The carburetor bolted directly to the top of the cylinder head with no separation or external intake manifold. What amounted to the intake manifold was cast directly into the head. I told Scott, "We've got to find a way to get more out of this Nash." The first thing we did was to take measurements of an eight-cylinder Nash Ambassador carburetor. We found it to have a quarter-inch larger throat diameter, so we made the opening in the head that much larger to match. The bolt holes had to be moved over too, and that was done without having it show. It was still all Nash and the performance was improved. It did turn up a little tighter. We found some larger intake valves that had the word "Nash" forged right on them, so we shortened the stems and made new keeper grooves as well as opened up and polished the intake ports. Once we had the bigger intake valves in place, we'd gained quite a bit more. We decided if we ever got the Nash going real good, we'd have to cool it and just not run away and hide from the competition. I don't think we needed to worry a whole lot about that. The next race, we got a second or a third in a field of strong cars.

The Nash had a somewhat lower compression ratio than most of the other stock cars of that time—about five-and-a-half-to-one, I think it was. So, when we found some bigger Nash pistons that could be adapted, and that would give about seven-and-a-half-to-one, we went ahead. The new pistons had domed heads, so we had to re-size them slightly and open the bore about 1/8 of an inch. Once we did that to the Nash, it was better still.

By this time, we were getting a little factory support. The parts were free and they were paying for my time spent on the car.

A fellow named Smallwood used to come around the Nash garage and help us work on the car. He had a friend, Tibbits, who had a contract to furnish two-way short radio communications for the crews working on the Golden Gate Bridge. Smallwood's idea was to get hold of some of this equipment so we could talk between the pit and the car during a race. This sounded like a great idea to me, and I agreed to try it. Tibbits came over and figured out where and how to install the equipment that was needed in the car. He said he would do this at no cost, believing that his communication's business would benefit from the advertising value of it. Regulations at the time required that one other person and I pass a test to be able to broadcast back and forth over the air. Scott Neilson was the one who would operate from the pit. We both went over to Frisco and passed the test with flying colors.

There were a couple of blank spots out on the track when we got to working with the radios, but we got along O.K. In that race, I was going to be running with a bunch of those quick Fords. I knew from experience that they'd be steaming like tea kettles after fifteen laps or so. When the flag dropped, they really took off, but I didn't let that get me all upset. About the third lap, Scott called me on the radio and said, "Herk, you'd better get going. Those Fords are blowing right by you." "Yah," I said, "that's alright, let 'em go. We'll see them later." After about fifteen laps, I went past the pits and saw three of them sitting there spouting steam like Old Faithful! I called in on the radio and said, "Scott, look at those damn Fords boil now, would you!" I forgot that my profanity was going out over the air, and that was against the law. The guys worried that we might get into trouble over it. All of us got quite a kick out of that whole episode, and it just might have been the first time a two-way radio was used in a race car.

There was an old airport outside of Los Angeles called Mines Field. A road racing course had been laid out on it, and when a stock car event was scheduled, we decided to go down with the Nash. Freddie Agabashian was also going to run and would be going down with one of his friends. We decided to start out from Oakland together, and Merced was a dinner stop for us. When we got on the road again, Freddie was running back of us. Buzz Taylor was riding with me, and he was quite a gadgeteer. He'd hooked up an exhaust gas analyzer and he wanted to do some high speed analyzing. It was getting along towards evening, and we were on a long straight stretch of road between Merced and Madera. "Open her up," Buzz said, "I want to see what she does at high speed." We were batting along at over 100 miles an hour—wide road and no traffic. I looked up in the rear view mirror and remarked, "By gosh, that Freddie is sure right on our tail, isn't he?" Buzz turned around and looked out the back window. "Sure is" he chuckled, "But Freddie's got some red lights flashing behind him."

"Oh boy!" So I shut off the key, coasted to a stop, and so did Freddie. The race numbers were already on the cars, and when the highway patrolman came up to look us over he said, "Don't you guys know that the race hasn't started yet?"

I looked at him and saw his name on a badge over his shirt pocket and asked, "Aren't you so and so's brother?"

Little, Big and Bigger

"Why, yes," he answered and added, "You used to go with my sister didn't you? I thought I recognized you."

We had a brief conversation and then got down to the serious business. "If I give you both a ticket, I know just what will happen. When you get to Fresno, you'll give them to Sprouts Elder and that will be the end of that." Sprouts Elder was a motorcycle racing champion, and at that time he was also on the highway patrol. "I'm going to let you guys go. Just take it easy, at least until you're out of my territory. If you see me out here on your way back, stop and let me know how you made out." We made the rest of the trip to Los Angeles without incident.

We had a connection with a Nash dealer in L.A., and when we pulled in there, we were welcomed with open arms. We weren't there very long when we heard that the race had been put off for a week because of the threat of bad weather. Buzz and I couldn't afford to hang around there for a week, so the Los Angeles Nash dealer came up with the bright idea of leaving our car on display in his showroom as advertising for the week. He offered us the use of a loaner and one hundred dollars, on the side, when the race was over. We took him up on the deal and returned to Oakland. When we got back down to Los Angeles the following week, driving the loaner, we put some new rubber on the race car and got it out to the track.

This was not going to be the first race that was ever held at Mines Field. They did decide, however, to change the shape of part of the course to make it more demanding and exciting for the spectators. When they got through, they ended up with a sort of "B" shaped layout. After the main straight, you'd make almost a complete turn, then a short straight within 100 yards and parallel to the pits, followed by another almost circular turn which hooked up with the other end of the main straight. It was the screwiest race track I ever saw in all my life.

We had everything on the car set up the way we thought it should be, so we went out for warm-up and a little practice. It seemed like we were getting that old dog around there pretty good.

The Bobby The Babe and Me

The shop foreman of the Nash garage in L.A. had made a deal with us that his brother-in-law was to be with me as riding mechanic, something the promoters had set up for just this race. Not too long before the race was to start, we're still waiting for the brother-in-law to show up. At the last minute, the foreman rushed up to us—all out of breath and full of apologies. The foreman's sister had found out about it, put her foot down and wouldn't even let this poor fellow come to the race. So, I had to pick up another guy, real quick, to ride with me. I needed Buzz to be in the pit.

The original surface of the track was O.K., but the second you hit the soft new stuff the car dug right in. I'd only gone a couple of laps when I lost a wheel. The car kept on moving, so I thought I might as well try to get back to the pit, and I did. Buzz spotted us coming in and answered my question as we slid to a halt. "How bad is it?" I yelled. "Oh! crap," he shouted, "You just broke the wheel right off. The nuts and center section are still on the hub." He got the old wheel center off and hung on a new wheel. Buzz came up with some big washers and put them under the nuts to stiffen the wheel center. As I was going out again he said, "Take it a little easy going into that first turn, Herk, and watch out for those holes." I tried to, but I'd only gone a few more laps and another wheel broke off. We used up all of our spare wheels and some that we'd borrowed from other Nashes sitting around. We still finished the race minus a wheel and running on the brake drum. A lot of other cars dropped out due to the punishment they were taking, and Buzz thought we should hang in there and try to finish. We had three wheels and no brakes and wound up in fifth or sixth at the end. I'd have to call that event a fiasco, and it didn't do much good for the Nash's image either.

We got the car back to the Nash garage in Los Angeles to put on a new brake drum and pick up one hundred dollars. The boss, flat out refused to honor the deal. "No" he said, "All I got out of that was a bunch of bad publicity." Maybe he thought he was entitled to an outright win at the track, but we didn't understand the terms that way. We put forth our best arguments, but he wouldn't change his mind. He just, absolutely refused to give us that one hundred dollars and that was that.

Another thing that took place at the Mines Field stock car race turned out to be rather unusual. A brand new Chevy sedan showed up with a couple of young-looking fellows in it. This was a car with an all steel roof, and that was a new feature in the General Motors line. They called it the "Turret Top." The officials, though a little short of cars, were somewhat leery of letting the kids run. They went around and talked to all the drivers and there were no objections. So the Chevy was let out for practice and the young fellows were doing O.K.—not having or causing any problems. A short time after the race began, the Chevy missed a turn and rolled off the course. That "Turret Top" was really put to the test. Too bad the General Motors people couldn't have caught that with their cameras rolling. That would have been an excellent plug for their new top. It rolled like an empty paper sack. Just rolled and rolled like it was never going to stop. When it did there wasn't a panel on the car that wasn't wrinkled, but fortunately, neither of the kids were hurt.

Charlie Currier had come down from Oakland to watch the race, and he later told me the rest of the story. These kids' parents had gone on vacation and left the new car locked up in the garage. Those kids, neither of whom were quite old enough to have driver's licenses, got the car unlocked, running and out on the street. When they heard about the event coming up at Mines Field, they decided they were ready to become race drivers. Maybe they thought they were going to do their folks a good turn and win enough money to pay off the mortgage.

When the parents got home, they came to the race promoter and really raised hell. They threatened to take him into court, but I never heard what the final outcome was of that episode. I just think about how lucky those kids were not to be hurt—no seat belts or anything like that. They must have really rattled around in that car while it was rolling like it did.

The Bobby The Babe and Me

We didn't see the speed cop on the way home. That was just as well. He probably would have expected better from us based on how we'd been going on the highway on our way down.

Seems like we were still doing better, overall, at the race track with the Nash than Scott Neilson was doing with his business. Some corporate reorganization was taking place at Nash and auto racing fell clean off their list of priorities.

A financial expert named Chet Jordan bought the Nash dealership from Neilson, and things began to change fast. He didn't go for that racing business or any other kind of similar foolishness at all. We called him "old money bags" when he wasn't able to hear it. He'd walk around with his hands in his pockets, looking at everything with a sour face and saying nothing to nobody, so it was no surprise to us when they sold the Nash stock car that we'd been racing.

Herk Edwards in a 4 port Riley at the Oakland Mile in 1936.   (Edwards Collection)

Herk Edwards at San Jose in 1931 driving Hap Howard's single stick Fronty.   (Bruce Craig)

Herk Edwards in Joe Armstrong's 4 port Riley at Oakland in 1936.

This Portland, Oregon car was not a memorable ride.

(McLellan Collection)

Herk Edwards in Paul Culp's Scoville Spl. at San Jose's 5/8 mile track.

(McLellan Collection)

Roy Canright standing at the cockpit with Herk.

Herk Edwards in Paul Culp's "SR" Fronty.   (Edwards Collection)

Herk Edwards in the Miller Scofield at Marysville in 1937.   (Edwards Collection)

Having A Ball

Charlie Currier was originally associated with Linn Mathewson in the building and promotion of the Oakland Speedway, a one-mile, high banked, oiled-dirt oval that was very fast. It went into operation in the fall of 1931 and was torn down during World War II. I didn't have much contact with Mathewson, but I did get to know Charley quite well. He was a fine gentleman. I don't know of any race driver who ever left his race track broke. He'd ask you how you'd made out, and if you were down on your luck, he'd slip you a five dollar bill and fill your gas tank.

Later on when I was out of racing and working in Alaska, I'd come down each year to winter in California. On one of those trips, I met Charley again at a Sunday indoor midget race he was promoting in the Oakland Auditorium. He was sure glad to see me and took me up into the press box. There I met a race driver from back east named Tommy Hinnershitz and an old-time movie cowboy named Hoot Gibson. I don't know if Gibson was a Canadian or not, but he was tied in with the Calgary Stampede somehow.

In between events on the track, we got to talking about a variety of racing subjects including the Mexican Road Race. When Hoot found out I had an Alaskan connection, he began asking me all about the Alcan Highway and related matters. Seems Charley and Hoot had it in mind to take the Mexican Road

Race, run it through parts of the Pacific Coast states, Nevada, Western Canada on the Alcan Highway, and end it at Fairbanks, Alaska. They made a list of things they wanted me to try to find out for them. As a result of working on that list, I came up with a tentative deal on a car for me to drive. Well, that caper died before it was born. I got a letter from Charley Currier later, saying that they had been working on the arrangement from his end. The plan was coming together fine, until they got to the matter of the Canadian border—that was the end of it. The Canadians wouldn't even discuss it. So, I didn't get to drive in the Mexican, American, Canadian Road Race because it never happened.

It was the Friday afternoon before a stock car race at the Oakland Speedway, and I was working at the Nash garage when a fellow and his girl friend drove up in a nice-looking 1937 Packard 120 coupe. He came in asking for me, and when I was pointed out, he asked if I had ever driven a car like his. I told him I hadn't. Then he began putting a lot of questions to me, in general, about stock car racing, especially the financial end of it. He also wanted to know if I was interested in taking over the car and running it in a race. I told him, "Sure, but you know how it is— I might take it out there and have something happen to it— bust it up or some darn thing." He said, "To tell you the truth, I'm in kind of a low spot right now, behind in the car payment, and the finance outfit is about ready to snatch the car. I really don't give a damn, and if there's a chance to make a few bucks out of it, let's go ahead." I agreed, and we made a deal. I told him I'd get a few sponsors lined up so we'd have some new tires, shocks and a few other little items. I gave this fellow bus fare so he and his girl friend could get back over to Frisco. I found out later that he was a professional gambler, and that pretty well explained why he was making those moves.

Smallwood and a couple of the guys that worked in the pit for me came in later, and I told them about the deal I'd made. They wanted to know if I thought the car would be competitive. I told them the only way to find out was to take it over to the track in the morning and try it out. I had a key to get in over there.

We didn't do a whole lot to the car on Friday evening. We drained the cheap gas and put in some high octane-leaded fuel. It needed better tires and our tire sponsor came up with new ones. We drained and replaced the motor oil and checked the grease in the transmission and rear axle.

When we put the car on the track Saturday morning, I was never so pleasantly surprised in all my life. The thing handled like a race car and really scooted. It had a very good coil spring front suspension with radius rods going forward to the frame from lower "A" arms. When I came off the track I told the fellows, "By golly, I think we've got something here." So we went to work on the car. We wanted to put some extra shocks on the back, so the fenders had to come off. This was a safety related change, so it was acceptable. The front fenders were left in place. Extra tires and wheels were needed, and we came up with those. I got hold of the Champion Spark Plug man, who was always very helpful. I asked him what heat range plug he thought we should use and could he get some of those for us? After he'd had a chance to check it out, he got back to me and said, "Herk, we're in trouble. The Packard has those little 8mm plugs and I can't come up with any of them here in the heat range I think you should be running." He had plenty of those that the car had come with.

At the time the rules for stock cars were that you had to use pump gasoline and they had a pump right there at the track. We had to do something about that. Previously, I had the fellow who did our radiator work build us a six-gallon dump can with a cover and perforated false bottom. We'd throw a gallon of benzol in there and then go over to the track pump and get our five gallons of gasoline.

Word got around that there was going to be a Packard 120 in the race on Sunday, and someone at the finance company got curious. They had a loan payment overdue on such a car. Charley

Currier came over to our pit on Sunday morning and told us the finance company men had been over at the pit gate wanting to get in and grab the car. They were making a lot of noise about it. Charley found out that the amount overdue was only thirty dollars, so he paid the thirty and told them to call off their dogs. That satisfied them and they left.

Charley figured he was getting more than thirty dollars' worth of good publicity from the Packard entry. Had he not been cooperative with them, the newspapers might have got hold of it, and that wouldn't have been so good. Charley reacted good-naturedly to the incident, which said a lot about the great guy he was.

The race was a 200-miler with a minimum of three pit stops. I think they wanted to create a little extra excitement for the fans with those mandatory stops. Freddie Agabashian was driving a Chrysler that day, and there were some of those "hot" Ford V-8s entered too. I was just about a second faster than the fastest Ford in qualifying, Freddie turned out to be about the only real competition. It looked like it was going to be our day. After a while, I had a whole lap on Freddie. When we had to make the first mandatory pit stop, I gained a half-lap more. Then we were driving exactly opposite each other on the track, and I could set my pace according to his. Despite what he might do, I was able to maintain that distance—speed up when he did and slow down when he did. I came in for fuel on my second pit stop, and I could tell from the look on Smallwood's face that something was wrong. He should have looked happy the way we were going. We had set a new track record for the distance and were sitting pretty. "Herk," he said, "We're in trouble. I couldn't get any benzol into this last batch of gas. Maybe you'd better ease up a little." After I got out and ran a while, the engine began to blubber. It must have been around the 180-mile mark. I thought, hell, I've got a lap and a half on Freddie; I'll just go in and get new plugs. I've got to make one more stop anyhow. I signaled the pit, came in on the next lap, and they began to change the plugs. They were doing that when Smallwood raised up from under the hood with a spark plug in his hand and a shocked look on his face. That car had an alloy cylinder head, and when that spark plug came out, it brought the aluminum threads right with it. So that was that. I yelled to Smallwood, "To hell with it! Leave it out. I'll run on seven cylinders." I went back out, and Freddie caught on right away. He got on that Chrysler, went by me with no trouble and won the race.

I'll never forget the ride I had in that Packard. When the Oakland Speedway was shut down and taken out, sometime later, I still had the stock car record for several distances and I guess I still do.

After the race, we put the Packard back in shape. I took the head off and had the machine shop drill and tap it for the next larger size spark plugs. We put the rear fenders back on. The dealer that furnished the tires let us keep what was left of them. The gambler had left a telephone number where we could leave a message, and we did that when the car was all cleaned up and ready. When he came in, we split up what little proceeds there were per our agreement. He left happy about the whole thing, and I never saw him or the car again.

A little later, a promoter was in town from Portland, Oregon. He stopped and wanted to know if I could get hold of that Packard for a race in the Portland area. He would have paid pretty good appearance money if I'd run it up there. I tried to get hold of the gambler again, but wasn't able to make contact. Too bad!

The next hook-up I made was with a fellow that had a Ford V-8 stock car. When I raced against the Fords, I saw enough of them with cooling trouble to get me to thinking about what could be done about that. The friend with the radiator shop told me he could build a radiator for that Ford that would help the cooling problem. He put one together that was just a little bigger with an extra set of tubes in it. He did such an expert job of it that no one ever caught on.

Another thing I tried was to use salt water as a coolant.

Someone had told me that salt would raise the boiling point as well as lower the freezing temperature. We had a ten-gallon milk can in the pits with a lid on it full of salt water. A blow torch was used to keep it warm so if we should have to add any during a race, we wouldn't damage the engine. On the day of the race, we would drain the system and put in the salt solution. After the race, we'd drain and flush the system and put plain water back in. We always kept the lid on the can to keep anyone from dipping in a finger and giving it the taste test.

Fred Frame gave me a good tip one day. He said, "You know, Herk, I've had some experience with those Fords." He'd driven one in the Elgin Road Race and in some other races too. "I'll give you a little advice that might help you out, but you have to watch your temperature gauge carefully. When you're out there running it hard, you keep your foot in it until the gauge gets right up there to the red line. Then you back off just a little—a few miles an hour. When you see the temperature starting to come back down, you get right back on it and run it up to the red line again. When you give it a little rest like that, you can run without boiling." With my own key for getting into the Oakland Speedway, I tried those things, and everything I did helped. Between the radiator, the salt water, and what Fred Frame had told me, I could hold the Ford together for a long race. I was doing O.K.

I left the Nash dealership in Berkeley after the race-oriented owner, Scott Neilson, sold out to the new owner who had no interest of any kind in auto racing. Working there, life became a little too drab and hum-drum for me, so I left.

Around 1937-38, I was driving a Harley-powered midget at the Emoryville races for an ambulance driver named McFee. It was there that I got to know Joe Banzai, who was head of the midget association in Emoryville. One day he approached me and said, "Herk, you're not doing much right now; why don't you come up to Lake Tahoe with me? I've got a deal going to work on the Roos brothers' speed boats." Those brothers were owners of a large department store in San Francisco and very wealthy is what they also were. Joe said we could stay at their place, work on the boats, and pick up a few bucks. It was his idea to borrow McFee's Harley midget and hook it on behind. There were to be 4th of July midget races coming up at Weed, near the California-Oregon border, and we could take that in when we finished with the boats.

We loaded everything and headed for Tahoe. The brothers owned two Chris Crafts and a Gar Wood. Joe had made a number of earlier trips up to Tahoe, so he became known around there as a guy who worked on boats and motors. Tahoe is at about 7,000 feet elevation. When the little guys with their outboards would come up from the valley, their motors wouldn't have the same old zip. They'd come over to Joe for help and he'd tell them, "Can't do it for you right now; we're busy with these inboards. If you want to leave it here, we'll look at it tonight." When the first of those guys left his motor and took off, I asked Joe what he planned to do. "Well," he said, "I'll show you later, but I can tell you this. Right now, we're going to pick up a little extra money here." Joe had templates for a bunch of different propeller blades. He just took a little material off the edges of those blades, filed them down and made them smooth again. When he took the motor out to try it, it would rev right up. What he was doing was similar to changing the gear ratio in the final drive. He was charging from ten to fifteen dollars for that, and we had a couple to do each night. He always told those guys the same story—he had to adjust this and had to adjust that. He never told them what he'd actually done. That was his little secret.

When we finished with the boats at Tahoe, the next stop was Reno to see one of Joe's gambling friends from Emoryville. We spent the night there, had a real good time and didn't get to bed very early—more like early the next morning.

On our run up to Weed, we stopped at Susanville and went through a lot of beautiful country along the way. I was pointing out the different kinds of trees to Joe, and he wanted to know how I could tell a Sugar Pine from a Douglas Fir from an Apple Pine.

I told him that when I was a kid, I'd worked a season up in the mountains—in woods just like these.

We arrived at Weed a few days before the race, so there was time to do a little laying around. Joe had his connections in Weed, too, and we were put up in the Weed "Hilton." The car and trailer with the race car on it were parked in front for whatever advertising value that might be. About the second day we were there, Joe got word that they wanted us out at the track. It had just been finished, the newspaper guys were there from the local Gazette and they wanted a little action. So we went out to turn a few laps for them. When we got there, we could see the track wasn't much of a track. They hadn't done any more than knock off the bumps with a grader.

So I took the car out and ran it a few laps, brought it in, lifted the hood and proceeded to fool around with it. There was nothing wrong with the car, but we were trying to make a little media event out of it. So I took it out again, ran a few laps, brought it in again and tinkered with it some more. We made a little something happen for those news guys, and I suppose they appreciated it.

A local kid was hanging around, like kids will do, all wrapped up in the car, and showing some hero worship that really wasn't called for; but then I remembered myself at that age. I had noticed a couple of nice-looking gals sitting over in the little grandstand, so I asked this young man who they were. He told me they were nurses from the local hospital. I asked, "Do you know them?" "Sure," he said, "do you want to meet them?" Smart kid—indeed I did! He took me over and made the introduction. I asked them if they were coming to the races on the 4th. They certainly were. Their boss had given them tickets, and they were looking forward to it.

After I returned to the hotel and got cleaned up, I decided to have something to eat at a small restaurant several blocks down the main street. I was walking along, not paying much attention to anything, when the horn of a car parked at the curb went "AH-

OOO-GAH, AH-OOO-GAH." I looked over at this Ford and saw a young lady sitting behind the steering wheel. "Can I be of help?" I asked.

"Yes, you surely can, if you're able to get this darn thing started for me," she answered.

"Well, if you'll just slide over, I'll have a try at it. Say, didn't I meet you out at the track this afternoon?"

"Why, yes. Oh yes, you're that fellow we met with the race car."

So I got in, turned the switch off, opened the throttle all the way and cranked it over a few times. Then I turned on the key, backed off the throttle some, cranked it over again and it started right up.

"Well, I'll be darned," she said.

"These Fords have a habit of flooding out like that," I told her. I explained the little routine to her again and went through the motions so she'd have it in mind the next time there might be trouble. I was a regular Boy Scout and helped a damsel in distress!

I told her I was just on my way to get something to eat. "Well, so was I," she said, "Let's go out to the airport. That's a nice place, and we can have a drink with our dinner." So we did, and she was very pleasant company.

The girls came to the race, and in the few days I was around there, we came to be quite well acquainted. Before I left, I told them about a big race that was coming up in August at Oakland and invited them down. I gave them the work address of my shop at 13th and Broadway, where I had an auto repair concession in a multi-storied parking structure. I told them to let me know if they were going to be able to make it. I was going with a girl in Oakland at that moment, and it was a kind of "on again, off again" deal. Looking ahead, I wasn't too certain what the situation was going to be.

The Bobby The Babe and Me

It was the Friday before the Oakland race. My girl friend and I were back together and I was expecting her to drop in so we could make plans for that evening. Things were busy in the shop and I was trying to wind up business before the day ended, when in drove this Ford all covered with red dust. I wasn't looking for more work that late on a Friday afternoon. There were a couple of gals in the car and they smiled and waved at me. I walked over to the car and HOLY SMOKE! OH BROTHER! It was those two gals from Weed.

Here we go!

They said they were sorry for not letting me know, but they decided to come down at the last minute. I was standing there talking to them and my girl friend pulled up to the curb. I'm telling you, if a guy ever wished he was some place else—that was me. I thought, What am I going to do now? Something inside said, "Keep cool, stay in control and make the best of it."

So when my girl friend came walking in, I called her over and introduced her to the two girls from Weed. The gals were real sharp and could see right off that I was in big trouble. They helped the situation by laughing about it and ribbing me. "What are you going to do now that you've got all these girls together in one place?" they asked. Everything worked out just fine. The two gals from Weed, Janet and Jinny, stayed with my girl friend, Betty, and the three of them went to the race together. We all had a great time and got to be good friends. They sure did have me in the "hot seat" for awhile. I guess I'd tried just a little too hard to earn my Boy Scout Eagle Badge up at Weed.

Back when I was getting started in the midgets, I got acquainted with a motorcycle man named Danny Muir. He had owned a cycle shop and was known for having built some very hot bikes. Danny could really soup them up. Later on, he went to work for the Fisher Body Company in Oakland as a machinist. Danny had got hold of a 100 cubic-inch, air cooled, Henderson motorcycle engine that he claimed was specially built for a speed record attempt. It laid around for a couple of years at his place until he and his brother-in-law decided to build a midget for it. It ran fairly good while it stayed together, but that it didn't always do. Danny continued to be interested in the car and traveled with it when he could get time away from his job. I drove the car some.

A number of races were coming up at Black Springs, Nevada, which was a little way out of Reno. This series was to be run on an old dog track, over an entire week, and would be set up with pari-mutual betting. Danny thought we'd be able to do alright over there, and I agreed to go along as driver. When we arrived, Danny re-carburetted the car because of the difference in altitude. He was very good at that sort of thing. When I went out for practice, he told me not to try to do my best, but just to go out there and play around a little. Danny was a betting man, and I figured he must know what he was doing. The starting grid was numbered, and we drew for starting position. Only one person was allowed to move between the track and the stands, and that was a highway patrol officer. The betting deal was going to be run just like they did for the dogs. Danny's wife and her friends were up in the stands, and she worked out some signals with Danny.

I went out the first night and won the race. That was fine. I did the same thing the next four nights and everyone was happy. On the sixth night, Danny came over to me and said, "Herk, whatever you do tonight, don't win this race! Spin out or do some damned thing; do anything but win." The race was about to start, and I had no time to ask any questions. I guess he planned it that way. I was out there running up front with Duane Carter when I realized that if I was going to do what Danny said, I couldn't wait much longer. So, I spun it out, limped back into the pit, and got out of the car. The highway patrol officer sort of ambled on by, had a few brief words, and slipped me a $100 dollar bill in the process. When the race was over, a number of others drifted by with similar, but smaller expressions of gratitude. Those were probably some of Danny's wife's friends. That was the last I ever saw of Black Springs. What we did was far from legitimate and a considerable distance from honest racing. I didn't feel very good about throwing the final race. What made me feel better was coming away with $1,200 total for the races we ran honestly. Danny and I split that down the middle. I didn't know what he pocketed from the betting he was doing at the track, but before we got back home Danny needed a loan from me! I got to hand it to the dogs, when they take out after the "Bunny"; they make the absolute, ultimate, genuine effort, and in spite of the money I felt lower than a dog for some time.

Ernie Lauck and Harold Mathewson were the Fresno midget promoters for awhile, and Ernie also built and owned a number of very fast midgets. Bryce Morris, a hometown favorite, was driving Ernie's outboard-powered car at the time. I had raced with Bryce quite a bit, and we got into a few bumping situations which were not at all serious, at least, we didn't think so.

There always seemed to be a need to have something to play up in the papers or talk about over the loud-speakers at the track—get the crowd worked up a little—good for the gate. This bumping bit was a lot like that, and I got to be the villain. They were coming down on me pretty hard and threatening to bar me, really playing it up. Sort of private-like, I was told not to worry about what I was hearing. Nothing was going to be done about it. This was the build-up for a match race between Bryce and myself. I got to be Herk "Tiger Boy" Edwards or something silly like that.

They got us out on the track and lined up for this match race. Bryce looked over at me, I looked at him, and he said, "O.K. 'Tiger Boy,' get your best hold on it 'cause here we go!" When we came around for the green, we were already banging into each other and just having a ball.

I don't recall which of us came out on top in that scuffle. The crowd would have been rooting for him, and maybe they weren't disappointed. Bryce might remember. He's still operating his truck parts business in the Fresno area and has that same little outboard midget on display at his place.

Herk Edwards in the Murphy car ready to do battle at San Francisco in 1937.

(Edwards Collection)

San Jose 1934. #11 Herk Edwards on the pole. Walt Davis outside. 2nd row outside "Reverend" Jack Menser.

Herk leads Les Dreisbach and Ted Horn at San Jose in 1931.

Herk in Roy Canright's Cragar at Oakland on February 5, 1933.

Herk Edwards leads Freddie Agabashian at the San Francisco Motor Drome in 1938   (Edwards Collection)

Pilgrims Rest Auto Park at Weed, California on July 4th 1938.   (Logan Collection)

The Keim and I

My next job was with the Ransome Company, located in Emoryville. This was originally a dirt moving and paving outfit. Eventually, they got into the bulk hauling business through the efforts of Ty Ransome, a son of the owner. That evolved into an interest in converting truck engines to using butane. They eventually got involved with anything that burned butane—torches, heaters, furnaces and what-have-you. They bought out a company called Forrester Burner & Torch, and took on those manufacturing operations. We had crews going out and installing furnaces we'd built. I took on the job of shop superintendent for the company. The general manager was "Pop" Schloss who had quite a background. He had been purchasing agent for General Electric back in Schenectedy, New York. He had been an Infantry Major in World War I and came out of that fracas with a leg injury that left him with a noticeable limp. He had also been manager of the Oakland Airport when it first opened. He then came over to the Ransome Company and stayed with them until he retired. He was an interesting old gentleman, and I remember him well.

Midget racing was enjoying an up-swing when Ransome Company put me on. A lot of fellows were attracted to the sport and were building cars for themselves that guys like me would drive. Everybody was doing his own thing; no two were alike. I got into quite a few of those cars, and most of them were junkers. A good car was hard to find.

The Bobby The Babe and Me

I was at work one day when "Pop" Schloss came over and said, "I hear you're fooling around with those midgets race cars." I thought, Uh-oh! Here we go again. There was no way I could deny it, so I confessed. "Where do you race?" he asked. I told him at Emoryville, Neptune Beach, and San Francisco. "When are the races held at Neptune?" he wanted to know. Well, Tuesday was the night, and when he heard that, he replied, "The next time you're going to race over there, let me know. Ty Ransome and I would like to see you race."

I had recently come up with a ride in a hot little car, called a "Keim." It was owned by Ted Antognoli of Fresno and had been built in Los Angeles. I'd set a track record with it at Fresno. That was before the two rival racing associations got into a big fight, and for jurisdictional reasons, I was temporarily prevented from running at Fresno.

When the race came up for Neptune, I let "Pop" Schloss know and told him I would pick up a couple of passes for him and Ransome. "No," he said, "No need for you to do that." That Tuesday night at Neptune, I really threw a fit. I set a new track record and had things pretty much my way. Between events, I was called over to the pit gate. "Pop" Schloss wanted to talk to me. "Find out if the owner wants to sell that car and what he wants for it," he said. I put the question to Ted Antognoli, and it so happened that such a move would work out well with his plans to get a new "Drake" powered midget. Ted told me the deal would not include the trailer he was using. The one he had that night was borrowed. His had wrecked, but he had another in Fresno that he would sell. Ted wanted my assurance that this boss of mine was serious. I told him "Yes" in a way that left no doubt. I went back to the pit gate and gave "Pop" the details. I told him about the trailer and he said, "Well, you guys in the shop could surely build one, couldn't you?" We sure could—we had all the facilities and equipment we needed. "Pop" said, "Tell Antognoli to stop by in the morning and we'll settle the deal."

The next day when Ted stopped by, "Pop" called me into his

office and asked what was required in way of a license, registration or title. I told him that a bill of sale with a detailed description of the car was all that was needed. Ted told us he had a lot of spare parts for the car in Fresno that he would give us the next time we got down his way. The "Keim" engine was developed from a four-cylinder 61-cubic-inch Henderson motorcycle motor. Johnny Keim had made patterns for a new 100-cubic-inch water cooled block, cylinder head and larger oil sump. The block and cylinder head were cast iron. The oil sump and the crankcase were aluminum. It was a very well-made engine and a credit to him.

After Ted left, "Pop" told me that the storage shed we had out in the back would be an ideal place to keep the race car and do the work on it. He didn't think it would look very good to have it sitting around in our main shop, and I agreed. "Pop" wanted to know what kind of a deal I usually got as a driver. I told him 50/50 and he said, "Well, that may have been alright in the past, but from now on you're driving for yourself."

I didn't get what he meant.

"The car's half yours," he responded to my puzzled look.

"How's that?" I blurted.

"Just what I said, half of it belongs to you now."

"Herk," said Pop, "you're running the shop. We've got fifty trucks running in and out of here, and if you can't dummy up race car parts to look like truck parts, you're not as smart as I think you are." That was the beginning of a memorable relationship.

One day Elsie Laird, our office manager, called me in to ask if I thought she'd believe that the 12-inch tires shown on the invoice she was holding in her hand would really fit on one of our trucks. I guess she wanted me to know that there wasn't much getting past her and have a little fun at the same time. She'd been around awhile and certainly knew her end of the business. She knew a little about midget race car tires, too.

The differences between two racing associations were soon settled and I was again able to race at Fresno. The fellows from down there would also come here and race on our tracks. We had a good circuit, and it improved the situation for all of us.

We built a nice trailer for the race car and had a good set-up on my passenger car for towing it. When we raced local, the guys in the shop were my pit crew. When we raced in Fresno, there were always fellows around who wanted to be part of the action. I was doing well with the Keim, but the Drakes were coming onto the scene, and they were getting better and better all the time. I was really reaching down into my bag of tricks to come up with things that would hold them off.

After every race with the Keim, we'd have to go over it and tighten every nut and bolt. There was a fellow named Casey Jones, who had owned one of the first Keims, and he told me that he'd experienced the same problem. His brother, "Skeets," had driven for him, and it had been a going machine. He solved the problem by making up two plates of half-inch ground steel, drilling and tapping the block and crankcase, on each end and then bolting the whole thing together. That made a single, stiffer, more solid unit. He said that he still had the template for the plates and if I wanted to use them, they were mine. When I finished the modification on our car, the improvement was noticeable right away. It ran smoother and didn't loosen up nearly as quick. It must have helped in other ways too.

After the season ended, I took the block and crank out to Wagner and Pagozzi, a high precision machine shop in East Oakland. They did a lot of aircraft and other high quality work. You almost had to be on a waiting list to get in there. I had some connections, so when I took the parts out to them they got right on it. The fellow there measured everything up and told me he couldn't find the slightest indication of any wear. He suggested I put it back together and run it. There was nothing he could do that would make it any better. Evidently, we had the right combination now.

When we first got the car, it was ready for another crankshaft. I got hold of a new forging and had it machined and ground. For balancing, we took it out to the Hall-Scott Company where we had friends. Our company had done work for theirs, and we knew they'd do a fine job. Between the stiffening plates and the new crank, we had a solid, reliable engine.

Another experience we had with the Keim was the rear end breaking loose coming out of a turn. This would happen at night at Neptune and San Francisco when the tracks cooled down. The surface would get hard and slippery—almost like ice. When the engine over-revved, it set up one hell of a valve clatter. There was a good chance of dropping a valve, and that's what happened several times. It tore up the whole package. Casey Jones had bought all the patterns and spare parts for the Keim, so I had to make a number of trips over to his place to pick up blocks, heads and whatever. Already, more had been spent for those parts than had been spent to buy the car originally. We weren't getting on top of our problem.

I'd heard that Joe Petrali, the motorcycle champ, was in town and I caught up with him at the Harley shop. He listened to me explain the problem, what I thought was wrong, and he agreed with me. He asked if I'd seen the internals of the new Harley engine. Well, I hadn't. He explained that they were using an inner valve spring now, inside the regular one. It was made of a little smaller wire and wound in the opposite direction, so the coils wouldn't catch. He had a couple of them to show me. He thought I might be able to get the springs and keepers I needed from Fred Offenhauser if I had all the dimensions. So, I figured out what I thought it would take and called the Offenhauser shop. They shipped me a set of springs, keepers and locks. I was able to redo the valve stems in our shop so as to receive the new locks and that took care of that. It had cost a bunch of money, time and points, but we started to go again.

The Ransome Company had an agency for the "Ensign" line of butane conversion equipment for automobiles. "Pop" got to wondering how butane would work out in a race car, and he thought we should try it. "Jeez," I said, "I'm making pretty good money with the Keim, I'm right up there in the point standings, and I'd like not to lose out on all that." He told me not to worry, I wouldn't come up short. They'd make up any shortfall that might come about as a result of this experiment. I don't know how any disparity in points was to be taken care of, but they had treated me very well and I felt that I had to go along with them.

So, to satisfy the boss's curiosity, we put butane on the race car. The Ensign Company was interested too—good publicity if it turned out to be a winner. Well, it wasn't a winner, and we tried everything we could possibly think of to get it going half-way decent. It never did, so we took the butane system off, returned to using our regular fuel, and gave up on the project. Butane was fine for trucks and passenger cars, but for race cars—forget it!

There was a fellow named Woody Cummings working at the Ransome Company, who was a sort of home-grown engineer. He was in the shop with me and had previous experience working on race cars. We had discussed the handling of the Keim midget and decided there was room for improvement. So, we brainstormed and built a fully independent rear suspension for it. Most of the parts came from the wrecking yard and the universal joints from a Plymouth drive shaft. The axle shafts were from Ford truck drive shafts. We used a Model "A" Ford center section to which we adapted a back plate for a single brake drum on the right side. What parts we couldn't adapt, had to be made from scratch. I guess, now, you'd call ours a "swing axle" design. At the time, we called it "knee action" for want of a better term.

Once we got it all put together, we needed a place to try it out under actual track conditions. There was to be an outlaw midget race up at Eureka, so that's where we went. The night before the race, we went over to their new-dusty track to test our novel suspension. I turned a few laps with it and came in. The car had really changed—now it ran like it was on rails and I couldn't get the back end to break loose or the engine to top out. It was like being glued to the track. I thought maybe we were going to need still lower gears than the five and one eighth to one "Taxi" gears we had in the car. Woody wasn't so sure, and besides, we didn't know of any lower gears being available.

We came back the following day for the race not knowing how it was going to work out. When the race got going, I was surprised how quick I was able to run away from those guys. I saw Woody standing down on the back straight giving me the signal to cool it, and I could see the wisdom of that. We didn't want to run away and hide. Why let the cat out of the bag right away? So, I was staying just ahead of the pack, when on the final turn of the last lap, the car took me right off the track and over the bank before I could do anything about it. I had no control whatever. When I was able to get back into the infield, Woody wanted to know what the hell happened. I told him I didn't know, but it was just like somebody had a rope on the front of the car and just pulled me straight off the turn. When we got the car up on the trailer, Woody said, "Herk, look here! This wheel is turning free. With a locked rear end, that can't be. Something's broke loose inside."

When we got it back to Emoryville and had a chance to tear it down, we found we had machined one side of the spool that carries the ring gear a little too thin. The part that drove the right side inner U-joint sheared off, and we'd lost power to the outside wheel. With all of the power put to the inside wheel, so suddenly, the car veered to the right, and there was no time for me to react. I just went along for the ride and got it shut down and stopped.

When we got the Keim repaired, we ran it at a number of other tracks, and it was working good on a fairly loose surface. Since Eureka, we found out that the car worked better if the tires had a rounded or curved tread section, especially on the outside of the right rear wheel. We went over to San Francisco for a race, and that particular night we were too much in a hurry and got things mixed up. Somehow we put new tires on with the square shoulders to the outside. It was a clay track, had been watered, and became very sticky. I went out to qualify, got into the first turn with my foot in it, and the outside tires just dug right in. The car went up and over and then just rolled and rolled and rolled. What it did was to roll me right into the hospital. It really did a number on me. It broke my left arm, right shoulder, four ribs on each side, and a vertebrae in my neck. Besides all of that, I had one big bruise—me!

Woody looked the turn over after the accident and could see where my outside rubber had cut into the track surface. The other guys blamed the accident on the independent rear suspension we were running. We didn't agree. Our concluding thought was that we were getting such good traction with our set-up that the engine never revved enough to be at peak power. In a sense, what we'd done was self-defeating. What was gained in one hand was lost in the other. How we would have worked things out had there been more gear ratios available is speculation. I'm sure quick-change rear ends would have made a big difference. They would also have increased the cost and raised the intensity of competition. Maybe we would have had the world by the tail, if even for only a little while.

I had guys tell me later, "You guys sure started something with that independent rear axle." I believe that what we did was already being done in Europe on their big cars. I'm quite sure that we were the first ones in our neck of the woods to try it on a midget race car.

The Drakes had gradually taken over, and there was no way we could hold them off. We kept dropping farther and farther behind in the points. Ransome's shop was busier than ever, and people there were losing interest. With war clouds on the horizon, there was talk of closing down racing nationally. So, the Keim, as with so many other race cars, was unceremoniously retired to its shed, and we all moved on to more serious matters. One era for the country was coming to a close, and a new, very serious one was about to begin. That was true for my life also.

The Keim and I

My World War II years were spent operating heavy equipment on government projects including the Alcan Highway and military facilities in Alaska. With the end of the war, I decided to remain in Alaska and continued to do similar work with my own equipment in the civilian sector. Eventually, I saw advantages in leasing my machinery to qualified operators while I continued to own and maintain it, so that's what I did.

Each year, I returned to California to escape those cold Alaskan months. I wintered in quite a few places up and down the coast and found Morro Bay to be the place that best suited me. When it became time to retire, I sold out in Alaska and returned to Morro Bay and settled in permanently. The ocean fishing is good, and that's where I am now much of the time. I make an occasional run over to Fresno to have lunch and bull sessions with some of my old racing friends.

In all of my years in racing there were none to compare to those spent with the Bobby and Babe Stapp. If I have any regrets, it would have to be not getting a chance to drive Charley Bobby's little "single stick" Fronty.

Bill Vukovich drove Ted Antognoli's "Keim" before it became Herk Edwards ride.

(Edwards Collection)

123

Herk Edwards in the "Keim"at the Fresno Airport Speedway in 1940.

(Lauck Collection)

Index

125

Index

Photo Credits

John Burgess
Bruce Craig
Herk Edwards Collection
Earl C. Fabritz Collection
Al Krause
John Kozub
Ernie Lauck Collection
Lloyd Logan Collection
Ed McLellan Collection
Leo McNamara Collection
Babe Stapp Collection
Ted Wilson

Herk Edwards in 1994

Herk Edwards